OXFORD Quick take off in

Italian

Francesca Logi

OXFORD
UNIVERSITY PRESS

OXFORD
UNIVERSITY PRESS

Great Clarendon Street, Oxford OX2 6DP

Oxford University Press is a department of the University of Oxford.
It furthers the University's objective of excellence in research, scholarship,
and education by publishing worldwide in

Oxford   New York

Auckland Bangkok Buenos Aires Cape Town Chennai
Dar es Salaam Delhi Hong Kong Istanbul Karachi Kolkata
Kuala Lumpur Madrid Melbourne Mexico City Mumbai Nairobi
São Paulo Shanghai Singapore Taipei Tokyo Toronto

Oxford is a registered trade mark of Oxford University Press
in the UK and in certain other countries

Published in the United States
by Oxford University Press Inc., New York

© Oxford University Press 2003

The moral rights of the author have been asserted

Database right Oxford University Press (maker)

First published 2003

All rights reserved. No part of this publication may be reproduced,
stored in a retrieval system, or transmitted, in any form or by any means,
without the prior permission in writing of Oxford University Press,
or as expressly permitted by law, or under terms agreed with the appropriate
reprographics rights organization. Enquiries concerning reproduction
outside the scope of the above should be sent to the Rights Department,
Oxford University Press, at the address above

You must not circulate this book in any other binding or cover
and you must impose this same condition on any acquirer

British Library Cataloguing in Publication Data
Data available

Library of Congress Cataloging in Publication Data
Data available

ISBN 0-19-860659-1 (Book and CDs)
ISBN 0-19-860658-3 (Book and cassettes)
ISBN 0-19-860736-9 (Book only)

1 3 5 7 9 10 8 6 4 2

Editorial: Mary O'Neill
Teaching consultant: Jenny Ollerenshaw
Copy-editing and proofreading: Susan Wilkin, Elspeth Anderson, Jane McCauley
Audio Production: Daniel Pageon, Actors World Production Ltd
Design: Paul Saunders   Typesetting: Pantek Arts Ltd
Series Editor: Natalie Pomier
Printed in Spain by Book Print S.L.

Contents

Introduction 4
Pronunciation guide 5

Quick Reference Section 7

Unit 1 – Greetings 17
- greeting people and introducing yourself
- talking about where people come from and where they live
- asking people how they are

Unit 2 – Eating out 31
- ordering something in a bar or restaurant
- asking someone what they'd like
- paying for your order
- asking for the bill and querying it
- counting up to 20

Unit 3 – Accommodation 45
- booking a room in a B&B over the phone
- checking in at a hotel
- finding out about campsite facilities
- making complaints and requests
- counting up to 1000

Unit 4 – Getting around 59
- catching a person's attention
- asking for directions
- asking about public transport
- asking the time and answering the same question

Unit 5 – Shopping 73
- shopping for food
- buying stamps, postcards and other items
- buying a present
- shopping for clothes

Unit 6 – Emergencies 87
- asking for help
- reporting a theft to the police
- asking for a doctor or an ambulance
- explaining that your car has broken down
- explaining that you've missed your plane

Answer key 101
Vocabulary 105
Grammar section and verb tables 119

Welcome to Quick Take Off In Italian!

Off to Rome for a weekend break or to Milan for a business meeting? Planning a romantic week in Venice or a skiing holiday in the Alps? Using this course, you'll learn enough Italian to be able to travel around and make the most of your stay. Learning to communicate in another language may be challenging, but it's also a very rewarding and enriching experience, and it's the best passport there is to discovering another culture.

A little language goes a long way

Even if you feel unsure about your ability to form correct, complete sentences, you'll find that it's possible to communicate with just a few words. Above all, don't worry about getting things wrong – people will still be able to understand you. They'll also appreciate the fact that you're making the effort to speak their language and they'll be all the more receptive. What's important is building up your confidence so that you're not too nervous of getting into conversations with native speakers.

When listening to recorded material, you aren't expected to understand everything the first time round. If you play the same piece several times, you'll most probably come away with something new each time. Learn to make maximum use of all the clues you can pick up. Listen closely to the speakers' voices. Do they sound happy, irritated, calm, etc.? We have left short pauses on the recording for you to repeat phrases or take part in conversations using prompts in English. These pauses are fairly brief but bear in mind that you can always pause the recording if you need more time to speak.

Using this course

You can use this course in two different ways. You can start with unit 1 and work through the six thematic units of the course. This will teach you the basics of the language through dialogues, activities and information on Italian usage. If you're in a real hurry or just want to brush up your knowledge of Italian, you can start with learning essential phrases in the Survival Guide and then dip in and out of the book by selecting the thematic units which are most relevant to your situation.

You will find the Survival Guide at the end of the second cassette or CD. You can listen to the phrases and repeat them while reading them on the credit-card size Survival Guide supplied with your pack. You can also use it

PRONUNCIATION GUIDE

for revision or to test yourself once you've completed the six units. The Survival Guide phrases can also be found in the Quick Reference section of your book, with some extra phrases.

When travelling, just slip it in your wallet or purse and you'll have all the essential phrases at your fingertips: from 'hello' to 'could you help me?', and from numbers to conversion charts.

At the end of the course, you'll find an Italian–English vocabulary list, a grammar section containing the terms marked with asterisks in the body of the course, summary tables and other grammatical information as well as verb tables. You'll also find an answer key, which contains answers to all the activities, except those found on the recording.

Pronunciation

Italian pronunciation is pretty straightforward and, with the exception of a few sounds, is not very difficult. Bear in mind that the whole of the word, i.e. each separate syllable*, is pronounced. Some letters such as the **vowels** or the consonant combinations ch and gh may take some getting used to at the beginning, but they'll become easier to pronounce with practice. You'll have the opportunity to listen to these sounds in the pronunciation section on the recording and to practise them throughout the course.

Vowels

In Italian, the vowels are always pronounced very clearly and are given their full value. The vowels **e** and **o** have an open and a closed variant each but since their pronunciation varies throughout the Italian regions, they shouldn't concern you too much.

Vowel	Approximate English sound	Examples
a	cat	pane, albergo
e (open)	let	bello
e (closed)	race	sera
i	easy	vicino, lunedì
o (open)	not	notte
o (closed)	rope	ora
u	good	uno, più

Where vowels occur together in a word, they are each given their full value and pronounced separately: aereo, piacere.

Consonants

Most consonants in Italian are pronounced as they are in English but note the following exceptions:

Written as	Approximate English sound	Examples
c + a/o/u or + consonant	cat	camera, come, cuscino che, crudo
but		
c + e/i	chimney	cellulare, ciao
g + a/o/u or + consonant	get	gamba, gola, guasto Inghilterra, grazie
but		
g + e/i	jump	gelato, oggi
gli	billiards	biglietto, figlio
gn	onion	signora, Bologna
h	*is silent*	hanno
	after c or g, it 'hardens' the sound	che, Inghilterra
r	*always rolled*	Roma, grazie
sc + e/i	ship	pesce, cuscino
z	its	stazione, grazie
	suds	zero

Double consonants

Where the Italian consonant is doubled (notte, tonno), the sound is lengthened somewhat along the lines of the underlined sounds in the English phrases 'bla**ck c**offee', 'whi**t t**ie', 'ga**s s**tove', 'to**p p**art' and so on. With the exception of **h** and **q**, any consonant can be doubled in Italian.

The alphabet

You'll have the opportunity to hear how to pronounce all the letters of the alphabet on the recording.

Stress

A common problem in Italian is to know where the stress falls in a word. Most Italian words are pronounced with the stress on the second-last syllable* (pizza, lontano), but for many other words, the stress can fall on the third-last syllable (camera, telefono) or on the final one. In this last case, there is a graphic accent on the final syllable (città, giovedì, caffè).

Quick Reference Section

The Quick Reference Section is the place where you can access those words and phrases that you're going to need in real-life situations while you're visiting Italian-speaking countries.

The section supports the course units but it can be used independently if you're in a hurry to learn key words and phrases for a particular occasion.

To help you, the section is organized in themes and gives you both the Italian and the English equivalents.

The Quick Reference Section can also be used for revision and as a means of testing what you've learned: just cover one column and see if you can find the correct translation. When a phrase is used in one of the course dialogues, the unit number is shown so that you can refer to the relevant section. You will also find essential phrases from this section on your Survival Guide and in the corresponding section on the recording.

Meeting, greetings, and saying goodbye

ciao	hi; bye	➤ unit 1
salve	hello	➤ unit 1
buongiorno	good morning	➤ unit 1
buonasera	good evening	➤ unit 1
buonanotte	good night	➤ unit 1
arrivederci	goodbye	➤ unit 1
a presto	see you soon	
a domani	see you tomorrow	
piacere	pleased to meet you	➤ unit 1
come sta/stai?	how are you? (*formal/informal*)	➤ unit 1
bene, grazie	fine, thank you	➤ unit 1
e lei/tu?	and yourself? (*formal/informal*)	➤ unit 1

Being polite

grazie	thank you	➤ unit 1
prego	you're welcome	➤ unit 3
per favore/piacere	please	➤ unit 2
scusi!	excuse me!	➤ unit 2
scusi!	sorry!	➤ unit 2

mi dispiace	I'm sorry	➤ unit 4
si, grazie	yes, please	➤ unit 2
no, grazie	no, thank you	➤ unit 2

Communicating

parla italiano?	do you speak Italian?	
un po'	a little bit	
non ho capito	I don't understand	➤ unit 1
non capisco	I don't understand	➤ unit 1
come, scusi?	pardon?	➤ unit 1
può ripetere, per favore?	could you say that again, please?	➤ unit 4
può parlare più lentamente?	could you speak more slowly?	➤ unit 4
come si chiama/ti chiami?	what's your name? (*formal/informal*)	➤ unit 1
mi chiamo …	my name is …	➤ unit 1
sono …	I am …	➤ unit 1
di dov'è/dove sei?	where do you come from? (*formal/informal*)	➤ unit 1
sono inglese/scozzese/gallese/ irlandese/canadese/francese	I'm English/Scottish/ Welsh/ Irish/Canadian/French	➤ unit 1
sono americano/-a, australiano/-a tedesco/-a, spagnolo/-a,	I'm American/Australian German/Spanish	➤ unit 1
sono di Londra/New York	I'm from London/New York	➤ unit 1
vivo in Gran Bretagna/ Irlanda/Scozia/ Galles/ Inghilterra/negli Stati Uniti	I live in Great Britain/ Ireland/Scotland/Wales/ England/in the United States	

On the phone

pronto?	hello?	➤ unit 3
chi parla?	who's speaking?	
sono Timothy Evans	it's Timothy Evans	
vorrei parlare con il signor/ la signora …	I'd like to speak to Mr/Mrs …	
posso lasciare un messaggio?	can I leave a message?	
richiamo più tardi	I'll call back later	
vuole lasciare un messaggio?	would you like to leave a message?	
lasciate un messaggio dopo il segnale acustico	please leave a message after the tone	
scusi, ho sbagliato numero	sorry, wrong number	
il numero di telefono	telephone number	➤ unit 3
il prefisso	area code	➤ unit 3

Accommodation

vorrei prenotare una camera singola/doppia	I'd like to book a single/double room	➤ unit 3
con bagno	with bathroom	➤ unit 3
ho una stanza prenotata per stanotte	I have a room booked for tonight	➤ unit 3
la prima colazione è compresa?	is breakfast included (in the price)?	➤ unit 3
cerco un campeggio qui vicino	I'm looking for a campsite/campground nearby	➤ unit 3
quanto costa a notte?	how much is it per night?	➤ unit 3
qual è l'indirizzo?	what's the address?	➤ unit 3

Changing money

dove posso cambiare i soldi?	where can I change money?
può cambiare i soldi alla banca	you can change money at the bank
qual è il tasso di cambio?	what's the exchange rate?
vorrei cambiare cento dollari/cento sterline in euro	I'd like to change $100/£100 into euros
c'è una commissione?	do you charge commission?

At the café

prego?	can I help you?, what can I get you?	➤ unit 2
vorrei ...	I'd like ...	➤ unit 2
cosa prende da bere?	what would you like to drink? (*formal*)	➤ unit 2
prendo ...	I'll have ...	➤ unit 2
due caffè, per favore	two coffees, please	➤ unit 2
pago ...	I'm paying for ...	➤ unit 2
quant'è?	how much is it?	➤ unit 2

At the restaurant

può portarci il menu?	could you bring us the menu?	
vorrei ordinare	I'd like to order	➤ unit 2
cosa consiglia?	what do you recommend?	➤ unit 2
com'è il pesce?	how's the fish?	➤ unit 2
sono vegetariano/-a	I'm vegetarian	➤ unit 2
non mangio la carne	I don't eat meat	➤ unit 2
sono allergico/-a a ...	I'm allergic to ...	➤ unit 2
come primo vorrei ...	as a first course I'd like ...	➤ unit 2
può portarmi [una forchetta]?	could you please bring me [a fork]?	
un coltello/cucchiaio	a knife/spoon	
un tovagliolo/bicchiere	a napkin/glass	

può portare un po' di pane/acqua/vino?	could you bring some bread/water/wine?	
cin cin	cheers	
il conto, per favore	the bill/check, please	► unit 2
insieme/separato	together/separately	
posso pagare con la carta di credito?	can I pay by credit card?	► unit 2
tenga il resto	keep the change	
il pranzo	lunch	► unit 6
la cena	dinner	
il piatto del giorno	today's special	

Menu reader

l'antipasto	starter, appetizer	► unit 2
il primo (piatto)	*first course*	► unit 2
la minestra	soup	
la pasta	pasta	
il riso	rice	► unit 2
il secondo (piatto)	*main course*	► unit 2
la pizza	pizza	
la carne	*meat*	► unit 2
il pollo	chicken	
il manzo	beef	
il maiale	pork	
l'agnello	lamb	
le salsicce	sausages	
la bistecca	steak	► unit 2
al sangue	rare (*meat*)	
giusto/-a	medium (*meat*)	
ben cotto/-a	well done (*meat*)	
fritto/-a	fried	
bollito/-a	boiled	
alla griglia	grilled	
arrosto	roast(ed)	
il pesce	*fish*	► unit 2
il tonno	tuna	► unit 2
il salmone	salmon	
le sardine	sardines	
le acciughe	anchovies	
i frutti di mare	*seafood*	
le cozze	mussels	

QUICK REFERENCE SECTION 11

i gamberi	prawns	
il granchio	crab	
l'aragosta	lobster	➤ unit 2
il contorno	*side dish*	➤ unit 2
le verdure	*vegetables*	➤ unit 5
l'insalata mista	mixed salad	➤ unit 2
gli asparagi (*plural*)	asparagus	
le melanzane	aubergines, eggplants	
i fagioli	beans	
i fagiolini	green beans	
i pomodori	tomatoes	➤ unit 2
i finocchi (*plural*)	fennel	
le carote	carrots	
gli zucchini (*plural*)	courgettes, zucchini	➤ unit 5
i cetrioli	cucumbers	
i porri	leeks	
le lenticchie	lentils	
i piselli	peas	
i funghi	mushrooms	➤ unit 5
le cipolle	onions	
i peperoni	peppers	
gli spinaci (*plural*)	spinach	➤ unit 2
le patate	potatoes	
le patate fritte	chips, (French) fries	
bevande	*drinks*	
l'acqua	water	➤ unit 2
gassata/naturale	sparkling/still	➤ unit 2
il succo d'arancia	orange juice	➤ unit 2
la coca	Coke®, Coca-Cola®	➤ unit 2
il vino rosso/bianco	red/white wine	➤ unit 2
lo spumante	sparkling wine	
la birra	beer	➤ unit 2
il caffè	coffee	➤ unit 2
il cappuccino	cappuccino	➤ unit 2
il tè	tea	➤ unit 2
il latte	milk	➤ unit 2
dolci	*desserts*	
la torta di mele	apple tart	
la crostata di frutta	fruit tart	
il gelato	ice cream	
la cioccolata	chocolate	
la panna (montata)	(whipped) cream	
la crema	custard	➤ unit 2

QUICK REFERENCE SECTION

gli spuntini	*snacks*	➤ unit 2
il panino al prosciutto	ham roll	➤ unit 2
il panino mozzarella e pomodoro	tomato and mozzarella roll	➤ unit 2
il tramezzino	sandwich	➤ unit 2
il toast	toasted sandwich	➤ unit 2
la brioche	croissant	➤ unit 2
le patatine	crisps, potato chips	
il sale/il pepe	salt/pepper	
lo zucchero	sugar	
l'olio/l'aceto	oil/vinegar	➤ unit 5
la maionese	mayonnaise	➤ unit 2
l'aglio	garlic	
la frutta e la frutta secca	*fruit and nuts*	➤ unit 5
la mela	apple	
l'albicocca	apricot	
l'ananas	pineapple	
il limone	lemon	➤ unit 2
l'arancia	orange	➤ unit 2
la pesca	peach	
il pompelmo	grapefruit	
la pera	pear	➤ unit 5
la susina	plum	
il lampone	raspberry	
la fragola	strawberry	
la ciliegia	cherry	
la banana	banana	
la noce	walnut	
la nocciola	hazelnut	
la nocciolina	peanut	
l'uva	grapes	➤ unit 5

What time of the day?

la mattina	morning	➤ unit 4
il pomeriggio	afternoon	➤ unit 4
la sera	evening	
la notte	night	➤ unit 3

When?

oggi	today	
domani	tomorrow	
ieri	yesterday	➤ unit 6
stamattina	this morning	➤ unit 1

stasera	this evening	➤ unit 6
stanotte	tonight	➤ unit 3
domattina	tomorrow morning	➤ unit 6
domani sera/notte	tomorrow evening/night	
domenica notte	Sunday night	➤ unit 3
ora/adesso	now	
presto	soon; *also* early	➤ unit 6
il fine settimana	at the weekend	
la prossima settimana	next week	

Telling the time

che ore sono?	what time is it?	➤ unit 4
sono le nove e cinque	it's five past/after nine	➤ unit 4
sono le nove e un quarto	it's a quarter past/after nine	➤ unit 4
sono le nove e mezzo	it's half-nine	➤ unit 4
sono le dieci meno venti	it's twenty to ten	➤ unit 4
sono le dieci meno un quarto	it's a quarter to ten	➤ unit 4
è l'una	it's one o'clock	➤ unit 4
è mezzogiorno	it's midday/noon	➤ unit 4
è mezzanotte	it's midnight	➤ unit 4
siamo in ritardo	we're late	➤ unit 4
siamo in anticipo	we're too early	➤ unit 4
parte alle tre di mattina/pomeriggio	it leaves at three am/pm	➤ unit 4
arriva alle ventuno e trenta	it arrives at nine thirty pm	➤ unit 4
comincia/finisce alle nove	it starts/finishes at nine o'clock	
apre/chiude alle sette	it opens/closes at seven o'clock	

Days of the week ➤ unit 3

lunedì	Monday	venerdì	Friday
martedì	Tuesday	sabato	Saturday
mercoledì	Wednesday	domenica	Sunday
giovedì	Thursday		

Months of the year

gennaio	January	luglio	July
febbraio	February	agosto	August
marzo	March	settembre	September
aprile	April	ottobre	October
maggio	May	novembre	November
giugno	June	dicembre	December

What's the weather like?

che tempo fa?	what's the weather like?
c'è il sole	it's sunny
fa caldo/freddo	it's warm/cold
piove	it's raining
c'è vento	it's windy
nevica	it's snowing

How I feel

ho fame/sete	I'm hungry/thirsty	➤ unit 2
ho caldo/freddo	I'm hot/cold	
sono stanco/-a	I'm tired	
sto male	I'm ill	➤ unit 6
ho mal di testa/denti	I've got a headache/(a) toothache	➤ unit 6
ho la febbre	I've got a temperature	➤ unit 6
mi sono fatto/-a male	I've hurt myself	➤ unit 6
mi fa male la spalla	my shoulder aches	

Emergencies

chiamate l'ambulanza	call an ambulance	➤ unit 6
chiamate la polizia	call the police	➤ unit 6
chiamate i vigili del fuoco	call the fire brigade	➤ unit 6
aiuto!	help!	➤ unit 6
al ladro!	stop thief!	➤ unit 6
al fuoco!	fire!	➤ unit 6
può aiutarmi?	can you help me?	➤ unit 6
ho bisogno di un medico/dentista	I need a doctor/dentist	➤ unit 6
cerco una farmacia aperta	I'm looking for a pharmacy that's open	
mi hanno rubato la borsa/il passaporto	my bag/passport has been stolen	➤ unit 6
ho perso l'aereo	I've missed the plane	➤ unit 6
ho un guasto alla macchina	my car has broken down	➤ unit 6

Directions

dov'è … ?	where is …?	➤ unit 4
scusi, per andare a … ?	excuse me, how do I get to …?	➤ unit 4
come ci arrivo?	how do I get there?	➤ unit 4
quanto ci vuole a piedi?	how long does it take to walk there?	➤ unit 4
è lontano?	is it far?	➤ unit 4
andare dritto	to go straight on	➤ unit 4

sempre dritto	straight ahead	
girare a destra/a sinistra	to turn right/left	➤ unit 4
tornare indietro	to go back	➤ unit 4
di fronte a …	opposite, in front of …	➤ unit 4
davanti a …	opposite, in front of …	➤ unit 4
in fondo	at the end	➤ unit 4
all'incrocio	at the crossroads	➤ unit 4
il semaforo	traffic lights	➤ unit 4
l'angolo	corner	
la rotonda	roundabout, traffic circle	➤ unit 4
il cartello	sign	➤ unit 4

In a shop

dica	can I help you?	➤ unit 5
vorrei vedere …	I'd like to see …	➤ unit 5
ha … ?	have you got …?	➤ unit 5
è un regalo	it's a gift	➤ unit 5
vorrei spendere meno	I don't want to spend that much	➤ unit 5
posso dare un'occhiata?	can I browse? can I look around?	➤ unit 5
posso provarlo?	can I try this on?	➤ unit 5
è (troppo) grande/piccolo	it's (too) big/small	
è (troppo) lungo/corto	it's (too) long/short	
da uomo/donna	for men/women	➤ unit 5
per bambini	for children	➤ unit 5
la taglia è giusta	it's the right size	➤ unit 5
è un po' caro/-a	it's a bit expensive	➤ unit 5
è bello/-a	it's pretty	
mi piace/piacciono	I like it/them	➤ unit 5
lo/la prendo	I'll take it	➤ unit 5
i colori	*colours*	➤ unit 5
verde	green	
rosso/-a	red	➤ unit 5
blu	blue	➤ unit 5
azzurro/-a	light blue	
marrone	brown	
giallo/-a	yellow	
nero/-a	black	➤ unit 5
bianco/-a	white	
viola	purple	
arancione	orange	
rosa	pink	

Numbers ➤ units 2 and 3

1	uno	25	venticinque
2	due	26	ventisei
3	tre	27	ventisette
4	quattro	28	ventotto
5	cinque	29	ventinove
6	sei	30	trenta
7	sette	40	quaranta
8	otto	50	cinquanta
9	nove	60	sessanta
10	dieci	70	settanta
11	undici	80	ottanta
12	dodici	90	novanta
13	tredici	100	cento
14	quattordici	101	centouno
15	quindici	200	duecento
16	sedici	300	trecento
17	diciassette	400	quattrocento
18	diciotto	500	cinquecento
19	diciannove	600	seicento
20	venti	700	settecento
21	ventuno	800	ottocento
22	ventidue	900	novecento
23	ventitré	1000	mille
24	ventiquattro	2000	duemila

Unit 1

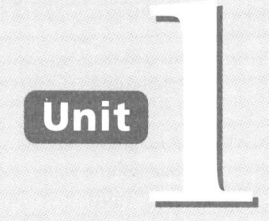

Greetings

In this unit you will learn how to:

- greet people
- introduce yourself
- talk about where people come from and where they live
- ask people how they are

When starting to learn Italian, be sure to work at your own pace. Make the most of the time available without trying to do too much all at once. You'll learn far more effectively by studying and practising frequently for short periods of time.

Unit 1 · GREETINGS

ACTIVITY 1 is on the recording.

DIALOGUE 1.1
- Ciao Anna.
- Oh, salve Roberto.

- Buongiorno signora.
- Buongiorno signor Paoli.

- Ciao Anna.
- Ciao Roberto.

- Arrivederci signora.
- Buonasera signor Paoli.

VOCABULARY

ciao	hi, hello; *also* bye
salve	hello
buongiorno	hello, good morning (*literally* good day)
signora	madam
signor Paoli	Mr Paoli
arrivederci	goodbye
buonasera	good evening; *also* goodbye (*used in the evening*)

Signore and **signora** mean 'sir' and 'madam'. They can also mean 'gentleman' and 'lady' in some contexts. When followed by a name, **signor Paoli/signora Vitti**, they mean 'Mr' and 'Mrs'. (Note how **signore** loses the final **-e** in this case). When addressing girls or young women, you use **signorina**, the equivalent of 'Miss'.

ACTIVITY 2

Listen to the recording and number the sentences below as you hear them.

___ Ciao.   ___ Buonanotte.   ___ Salve.

___ Arrivederci signora. ___ Buonasera.   ___ Ciao Anna.

___ Buongiorno signorina. ___ Arrivederci signor Paoli.

ACTIVITY 3 is on the recording.

DIALOGUE 1.2
- Ciao, sono Roberto.
- Ciao, io sono Anna.

- Caroline Scott, piacere.
- Piacere, Enrico Paoli.

VOCABULARY	
sono (verb essere)	I am (to be)
io	I
piacere	pleased to meet you

- When shaking hands with someone, you say **piacere**, which is short for **piacere di conoscerla** (*a pleasure to meet you*) and is slightly formal. You can say it before or after your name. In more informal situations, though, **ciao** is fine.
- As the dialogue shows, you can use both phrases – **sono Roberto** or *io* **sono Anna** – to say who you are. Pronouns* like **io** (meaning *I*) are sometimes optional in Italian. Later on in the unit, you'll see that it's the different verb* endings* which identify who or what is being referred to, whereas words like **io** are really used for emphasis.

ACTIVITY 4

Match each of the greetings in the left-hand column with the appropriate response from the right-hand one. Make sure that the level of formality/informality and the time of day match in each exchange.

1. Ciao, sono Caroline.   a. Piacere, Enrico Paoli.
2. Buongiorno, Enrico Paoli.   b. Salve, io sono Roberto.
3. Piacere, Roberto Castelli.   c. Buonasera, io sono Anna Torri.
4. Buonasera, Caroline Scott.   d. Buongiorno, io sono Roberto Castelli.

ACTIVITIES 5 and **6** are on the recording.

ACTIVITY 7 is on the recording.

DIALOGUE 1.3

● Ciao, io sono Roberto. E tu come ti chiami?
■ Mi chiamo Claudia.

◆ Buongiorno. Io mi chiamo Simona Vitti. Lei come si chiama?
◇ Buongiorno. Io sono Tom Hemshall.

▲ Tu sei Anna?
▽ Sì, sono Anna. Scusi, lei è il signor Paoli?
▲ Sì, Enrico Paoli.

VOCABULARY

e	and
tu	you (*informal, singular*)
come ti chiami?	what's your name? (*informal*)
mi chiamo	my name is
lei	you (*formal, singular*)
come si chiama?	what's your name? (*formal*)
sei (verb essere)	you are (*informal, singular*) (to be)
sì	yes
scusi	excuse me (*formal*)
lei è	you are (*formal, singular*)

- In Italian, there is an informal and a formal way of addressing people. The informal **tu** form takes the second person* of the verb* (see language note on page 25) – **(tu) come ti chiami?**; the formal **lei** takes the third person – **(lei) come si chiama?** Be careful because **lei** can also mean 'she'. However, when used as a formal singular 'you', **lei** applies to both male and female. (For more information on **tu** and **lei**, take a look at the Culture section on page 26).
- To ask questions, you can use question words* such as in **come ti chiami?** (later in this unit you'll come across **come stai?** and **dove abiti?**). Another very simple way of asking a question is to raise the intonation* of your voice at the end of a sentence, leaving the structure of the statement unchanged:

> **tu sei Anna** (you are Anna) becomes **tu sei Anna?** (are you Anna?). You'll have the opportunity to practise this in the audio activity.
>
> • In the previous dialogues, you've come across **(io) sono**, **(tu) sei**, **(lei) è**, the first three forms of verb **essere** ('to be') which is an irregular* verb. You'll find out more about verbs later in the unit. Look at the table below and work through the whole of the present tense*.
>
> | (io) | **sono** I am | (noi) | **siamo** we are |
> |---|---|---|---|
> | (tu) | **sei** you are (*informal*) | (voi) | **siete** you are |
> | (lui/lei;lei) | **è** he/she/it is; you are (*formal*) | (loro) | **sono** they are |

ACTIVITY 8

Match the following questions and answers. Remember to check whether the language is formal or informal.

1. Scusi, lei come si chiama?
2. Tu sei Caroline?
3. Lei è Enrico Paoli?
4. Ciao, come ti chiami?

a. Sì, sono Caroline.
b. Ciao, io mi chiamo Anna.
c. Mi chiamo Enrico Paoli. E lei?
d. No, io sono Roberto Castelli.

ACTIVITY 9

Some people are meeting for the first time and are busy working out who everyone is. Fill in the gaps using the correct form of the verb **essere**.

Io _____ Enrico. Tu _____ Caroline?

Noi _____ Fabio e Claudia.

Lui _____ Roberto e lei _____ Simona.

Lei _____ il signor Paoli?

Voi _____ Anna e Roberto?

Loro _____ Tom e Liz.

ACTIVITIES 10, 11 and 12 are on the recording.

Unit 1 · GREETINGS

ACTIVITY 13 is on the recording.

DIALOGUE 1.4

- Io sono italiano. Tu sei inglese?
- Sì, sono inglese.
- Di dove sei?
- Sono di Londra.

- Lei, scusi, di dov'è?
- Sono americana.
- Di dove?
- Di San Francisco.

- Voi di dove siete?
- Io sono inglese, lui è scozzese. E voi?
- Noi siamo italiani, di Roma.

VOCABULARY

italiano/-a	Italian
inglese	English
dove	where
di dove sei?	where are you from? (*informal, singular*)
di Londra	from London
di dov'è?	where are you from? (*formal, singular*)
americano/-a	American
scozzese	Scottish
Roma	Rome

- In the dialogue, you've seen **italiano** and **americana**. This is because there are two genders* in Italian, masculine* and feminine*, which means that adjectives* (and nouns*) have different endings*. In the singular*, adjectives with the masculine ending in **-o** take the feminine ending **-a** (**italiano/-a**). Those ending in **-e**, such as **inglese**, have the same form for masculine and feminine singular. This pattern applies to all adjectives. Take a look at the table on the opposite page to see how the masculine and feminine forms change when they become plural*.

	masculine	feminine		masculine	feminine
singular	italiano	italiana	plural	italiani	italiane
	inglese	inglese		inglesi	inglesi

- Italians often use **inglese** to refer to anything British – not just English. The correct term, however, is **britannico/-a**. If you want to specify where you come from in the British Isles, you can say you are **scozzese** (Scottish), **irlandese** (Irish) or **gallese** (Welsh).
- Note the difference between **dove** (where) and **dov'è** (where is). **Dove** loses the final **-e** and takes an apostrophe when followed by **è**. So you have **di dove sei?** but **di dov'è?** Listen out for the difference in pronunciation on the recording.

ACTIVITY 14

Listen to the recording and choose TRUE or FALSE for each of the following statements.

1. Dan è australiano.   TRUE/FALSE
2. Caroline è inglese.   TRUE/FALSE
3. Paul e Linda sono britannici. TRUE/FALSE
4. Mary è irlandese.   TRUE/FALSE
5. Ian è gallese.   TRUE/FALSE
6. John e Tony sono canadesi.   TRUE/FALSE
7. Io sono francese.   TRUE/FALSE

ACTIVITY 15

Fill the gaps with the correct form of the adjective indicating nationality.

1. Tom e Liz sono _____ . (British)
2. Io sono _____ . (Canadian)
3. Noi siamo _____ . (American)
4. Simona e Anna sono _____ . (Italian)
5. Lui è _____ . (Australian)
6. Siete _____ ? (French)

ACTIVITIES 16 and 17 are on the recording.

Unit 1 · GREETINGS

ACTIVITY 18 is on the recording.

DIALOGUE 1.5

- Liz, Tom, buongiorno! Come state stamattina?
- Bene, grazie. E lei signora? Come sta?
- Non c'è male, grazie. Siete irlandesi?
- No, non siamo irlandesi, siamo scozzesi.
- Dove abitate?
- Come, scusi? Non ho capito.
- Dove vivete?
- Aaah, ho capito! Abitiamo in Scozia, a Edimburgo.
- E lei dove abita, signora?
- Io vivo a Venezia. Sono qui in vacanza.

VOCABULARY

come state?	how are you? (*plural*)
stamattina	this morning
bene	fine
grazie	thanks
come sta?	how are you? (*singular, formal*)
non c'è male	not too bad
no	no
abitate (verb abitare)	you live (*plural*) (to live)
come?	pardon?
non ho capito (verb capire)	I don't understand (to understand)
vivete (verb vivere)	you live (*plural*) (to live)
ho capito	I understand
abitiamo	we live
in Scozia	in Scotland
a Edimburgo	in Edinburgh
Venezia	Venice
qui	here
in vacanza	on holiday/vacation

- Italian verb endings change along with each pronoun* (**io, tu, lei, noi** etc). English verbs change to a lesser extent so you have 'I live' but 'he lives'. In Italian you say **io abito, tu abit***i*, **lei abita, noi abit***iamo*, etc.
The best way to learn verbs is to think of them in groups. Whenever you look up an Italian verb in the dictionary, you'll find it appears in the infinitive* form (**abitare** = to live). Italian verbs fall into three main categories or conjugations*. The ending of each infinitive form will tell you which conjugation a verb belongs to. The three patterns for infinitive endings are: **-are, -ere, -ire**, as in **abitare, vivere, capire**. If a verb is regular*, the standard pattern of endings matching each pronoun can be applied to other verbs in the same category or conjugation. What you learn for the model verb is more or less valid for all other verbs in that category. This is also true of the verb patterns for the different tenses*. Many very common verbs are irregular* and it's best to learn them as you come across them. See the grammar summary for the tables of main verbs.

- To make a sentence negative, you just put **non** (= not) in front of the verb:
sono/non sono irlandese (I am/I'm not Irish)
loro abitano/loro non abitano a Roma (they live/they don't live in Rome)

ACTIVITY 19

Match the English with the Italian equivalent.

1. We are on holiday.
2. He isn't English.
3. I don't live in Rome.
4. Where do you live?
5. What are their names?
6. How are you?

a. Non abito a Roma.
b. Dove vivete?
c. Come si chiamano?
d. Siamo in vacanza.
e. Non è inglese.
f. Come stai?

ACTIVITY 20

Write the following sentences in the negative form, adding **non**.

1. Vive a Venezia.
2. Loro abitano in Scozia.
3. Siamo americani.
4. Ho capito.
5. Liz è qui in vacanza.
6. Si chiamano Hemshall.

ACTIVITIES 21 and 22 are on the recording.

Culture

One of the first differences you'll notice between English and Italian is the fact that Italians can choose to address people in a formal or an informal way. To do this, they use the pronouns **tu** or **lei** (along with the appropriate verbs) which both translate as 'you' in English.

Italians won't be offended if you get it wrong and they'll appreciate that you're making an effort to speak their language. But as this is an important feature of their culture, it will make a real difference if you understand a bit more about it and try to get it right.

Tu is used with family, friends, children and young people, and animals. It is also often used among work colleagues at the same level. **Lei** is used with people you don't know (or don't know very well), unless they are quite young. As a rough guide, assume that the under-20s are definitely '**tu** people' unless the conversational situation is clearly a formal one. You use **lei** with older colleagues and people who you think are entitled to particular respect. (There are lots of very young policemen, for example, with whom you should use **lei** as a sign of respect). Finally, although you'd address older blood relatives informally, you tend to use **lei** with in-laws or partners' families, at least at the beginning.

All this may sound complicated, but after a while it's easy to understand how it all works and get the hang of it. When you're not sure, it's always better to **dare del lei**, which means to use the **lei** form. If this feels too formal, the person you're talking to will say **diamoci del tu**, which means 'let's use the **tu** form' or **dammi del tu**, 'use the **tu** form' and you can even do so yourself if you feel you're in a position to do so.

ACTIVITY 23

Anna meets four different people and each time she's faced with the **tu** or **lei** dilemma. Listen to the four mini-dialogues on the recording and complete the grid below to indicate whether the conversations end up being informal or formal in tone.

	FORMAL	INFORMAL
1. Anna – Signora Vitti		
2. Anna – Signor Paoli		
3. Anna – Roberto		
4. Anna – Liz		

ACTIVITY 24

When Caroline meets Roberto, she's not sure whether to address him in a formal or an informal manner. They manage to sort it out between them. Fill in the gaps and complete the conversation.

- Buongiorno. Lei _____ italiano?

- Sì, sono _____ . Diamoci _____ tu.

- Sì. Come _____ chiami?

- Roberto. E _____ ?

- Caroline.

Review 1

1. Match the Italian with its English equivalent.

1. Salve.
2. Sono scozzese.
3. Di dove sei?
4. Abitano a Londra.
5. È italiano?
6. Dov'è?
7. Come sta, signora?
8. Siamo qui in vacanza.

a. Are you Italian?
b. They live in London.
c. How are you, madam?
d. I'm Scottish.
e. Where are you from?
f. We're here on holiday.
g. Hello.
h. Where is it?

2. Now match questions and answers.

1. Come ti chiami?
2. Come sta?
3. Dove abitate?
4. Di dov'è Sara?
5. Sei italiano?
6. Siete in vacanza?

a. No, sono francese.
b. È di New York.
c. Bene, grazie.
d. Mi chiamo Caroline.
e. Abitiamo a Venezia.
f. Sì, siamo in vacanza.

3. Following the example, write down brief introductions for the people below and then write one for yourself.

Mi chiamo Enrico, sono italiano e abito a Roma.

George/American/New York
Caroline/English/London
Claudia/Italian/Venice
Tom/Scottish/Edinburgh
Dan/Australian/Sydney

Time to listen

4. Listen to the recording and then fill in the gaps.

- Buongiorno _____ _____ Caroline Scott. E _____ ?
- _____ Io _____ _____ Roberto Castelli.
- Di _____ ?
- Sono di Bologna. Lei è _____ ?
- Sì, sono inglese.
- _____ vive?
- _____ a Londra. E lei? Abita qui _____ Roma?
- Sì _____ a Roma.

5. Listen to the three short dialogues on the recording and circle the correct answers below.

1) What nationality is she?
   a. She's French.
   b. She's American.
   c. She's Irish.
2) Where do they live?
   a. They live in Venice.
   b. They live in New York.
   c. They live in Rome.
3) Why are they here?
   a. They are on a school trip.
   b. They live here.
   c. They are on holiday.

Unit 1 · GREETINGS

Time to talk

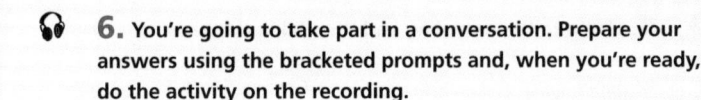

6. You're going to take part in a conversation. Prepare your answers using the bracketed prompts and, when you're ready, do the activity on the recording.

– Ciao.
(Say 'Hi')
– Come stai?
(Say 'I'm fine, thanks.')
– Come ti chiami?
(Say 'My name is …')
– Di dove sei?
(Say 'I'm American.')
– Dove abiti?
(Say 'I live in Los Angeles.')
– Sei qui in vacanza?
(Say 'Yes, I'm here on holiday.')

7. Now test your progress in Unit 1. How would you say:

a. my name is …
b. pleased to meet you
c. I'm from Toronto
d. what's your name? (*formal*)
e. are you Italian? (*plural*)
f. where are they from?
g. I'm not American, I'm Canadian
h. pardon? I don't understand
i. how are you? (*informal*)

You can check your answers on the recording.

Unit 2

Eating out

In this unit you will learn how to:

- order something in a bar or restaurant
- ask someone what they'd like
- pay for your order
- ask for the bill and query it
- count up to 20

There are many words that are very similar in Italian and English. When listening to the recordings, look out for those words that sound familiar. You'll be surprised how much you can understand even if you don't know every single word in the sentence.

Unit 2 · EATING OUT

ACTIVITY 1 is on the recording.

DIALOGUE 2.1
- Prego?
- Un caffè e una brioche.
- Una birra e un tramezzino tonno e maionese.

VOCABULARY

prego?	can I help you?
un caffè	espresso
una brioche	croissant
una birra	beer
un tramezzino	sandwich
tonno e maionese	tuna and mayonnaise

ACTIVITY 2 is on the recording.

DIALOGUE 2.2
- Anna, cosa prendi da bere?
- Vorrei un succo d'arancia.
- Qualcosa da mangiare?
- No grazie. Non ho fame.
- Io ho sete e ho molta fame. Prendo un bicchiere d'acqua gassata e un panino.

VOCABULARY

cosa prendi da bere?	what would you (*singular*) like to drink?
vorrei	I'd like
un succo d'arancia	orange juice
qualcosa da mangiare	something to eat
non ho fame	I'm not hungry
ho sete	I'm thirsty
ho molta fame	I'm very hungry
un bicchiere d'acqua gassata	glass of sparkling water
un panino	roll

> - Most Italian nouns* end in **-o** (**tramezzino, succo**), **-a** (**birra, acqua**), or **-e** (**bicchiere, maionese**). Unlike English nouns, they are either masculine* or feminine* in gender*. Usually, words ending in **-o** are masculine, those ending in **-a** are feminine and nouns ending in **-e** can be either (**bicchiere** is masculine, **maionese** is feminine). Nouns ending in consonants* (**bar, toast**) are masculine.
> - You may have spotted that 'a roll' is **un panino** while 'a beer' is **una birra**. In Italian, the indefinite article* (the equivalent of *a* or *an*) varies depending on whether the noun it is used with is masculine or feminine. You use:
> **un** before masculine nouns: **un toast** (a toasted sandwich), **un panino** (a roll);
> **uno** before masculine nouns starting with **gn-, ps-, z-,** or **s** + consonant: **uno spuntino** (a snack);
> **una** before feminine nouns: **una birra** (a beer);
> **un'** before feminine nouns starting with a vowel*: **un'acqua gassata** (a sparkling mineral water).

ACTIVITY 3

Match the following Italian sentences with their English equivalents.

1. Vorrei una coca.
2. Cosa prendi?
3. Un tramezzino e una birra.
4. Ho sete.
5. Prendo un bicchiere d'acqua.
6. Io vorrei un succo d'arancia.

a. I'd like an orange juice.
b. A sandwich and a beer.
c. I'll have a glass of water.
d. I'd like a Coca-Cola®.
e. What are you having?
f. I'm thirsty.

ACTIVITY 4

In the recorded dialogue, listen to four people ordering something to eat and drink in a bar. What do they order?

1. a) una birra b) un bicchiere d'acqua c) una coca
2. a) un tramezzino b) un toast c) un panino
3. a) un succo d'arancia b) una brioche c) un'acqua gassata
4. a) un panino e un bicchiere d'acqua b) una coca e una birra c) una brioche e un succo d'arancia

ACTIVITIES 5 and 6 are on the recording.

Unit 2 · EATING OUT

ACTIVITY 7 is on the recording.

DIALOGUE 2.3
- Pago un tè, due aranciate, tre cappuccini e quattro caffè. Quant'è?
- Quindici euro e dieci centesimi.
- Ecco a lei.
- Ha spiccioli?
- No mi dispiace, non ho spiccioli. Ho soltanto venti euro.

VOCABULARY

pago (verb pagare)	I'm paying for (*literally* I pay) (to pay for)
un tè	tea
un'aranciata	orangeade
quant'è?	how much is it?
un euro	euro
un centesimo	cent
ecco a lei	here you are (*formal*)
ha (verb avere)	you have (*formal*) (to have)
spiccioli	(small) change
mi dispiace	I'm sorry
ho (verb avere)	I have (to have)
soltanto	only

- Here are the numbers from 0 to 20. You'll have the opportunity to practise pronouncing them on the recording.

0 **zero** 1 **uno** 2 **due** 3 **tre** 4 **quattro** 5 **cinque** 6 **sei** 7 **sette** 8 **otto** 9 **nove** 10 **dieci** 11 **undici** 12 **dodici** 13 **tredici** 14 **quattordici** 15 **quindici** 16 **sedici** 17 **diciassette** 18 **diciotto** 19 **diciannove** 20 **venti**

- Just as noun* endings vary between masculine and feminine, they also vary between singular* and plural*.

Masculine nouns in **-o** change to **-i**: **un cappuccino/tre cappuccini**
Feminine nouns in **-a** change to **-e**: **un'aranciata/due aranciate**

> Nouns ending in **-e**, change to **-i**: **un bicchiere/due bicchier*i***
> Some nouns don't change in the plural. These are nouns ending in an accented vowel*(**quattro caffè**), in a consonant* (**due bar**), and exceptions such as **euro** (**venti euro**). There are also some irregular plurals which you'll learn as you come across them.
>
> ● In the dialogue, you've seen various forms of the verb **avere** (to have). It's an irregular verb*.
>
> | | | | | |
> |---|---|---|---|---|
> | (io) | **ho** I have | | (noi) | **abbiamo** we have |
> | (tu) | **hai** you have | | (voi) | **avete** you have |
> | (lui/lei; lei) | **ha** he/she/it has you have (*formal*) | | (loro) | **hanno** they have |

ACTIVITY 8

Match the English questions and phrases with their Italian equivalents.

1. I'm paying for two coffees.
2. How much is it?
3. Six euros and five cents.
4. Have you got any change?
5. Four euros and ten cents.

a. Quant'è?
b. Sei euro e cinque centesimi.
c. Pago due caffè.
d. Quattro euro e dieci centesimi.
e. Ha spiccioli?

ACTIVITY 9

On the recording, listen to Roberto checking the price of various drinks on a till receipt and then fill in the gaps.

1. _____ aranciata, _____ euro.
2. _____ coche, tre euro e _____.
3. Tre _____, _____ euro.
4. Un _____, _____ euro.

ACTIVITIES 10 and 11 are on the recording.

ACTIVITY 12 is on the recording.

DIALOGUE 2.4

- Volete ordinare?
- Sì, grazie. Non vogliamo l'antipasto. Come primo io vorrei le lasagne.
- Io prendo il riso allo zafferano.
- Come secondo la bistecca e come contorno gli spinaci.
- Io non mangio la carne, sono vegetariano. Cosa consiglia? Com'è il pesce?
- Il pesce è fresco, molto buono. Abbiamo anche l'aragosta.
- Aah! Voglio l'aragosta! E come contorno insalata mista.
- Cosa volete bere?
- Vino rosso e acqua naturale.

VOCABULARY

voglio/vogliamo/volete (verb volere)	I/we/you (*plural*) want (to want)
ordinare	to order
l'antipasto (*m*)	starter, appetizer
come primo	as a first course
le lasagne (*plural*)	lasagne
il riso allo zafferano	saffron rice
come secondo	as a main course
la bistecca	steak
gli spinaci	spinach
il contorno	side dish
mangio (verb mangiare)	I eat (to eat)
la carne	meat
vegetariano/-a	vegetarian
cosa consiglia?	what do you recommend?
com'è il pesce?	how's the fish?
fresco/-a	fresh
molto buono/-a	very nice
l'aragosta (*f*)	lobster
l'insalata mista	mixed salad
il vino rosso	red wine
l'acqua naturale (*f*)	still mineral water

- Like **un/una**, the definite article* ('the' in English) changes according to the gender* of the noun* it precedes. With masculine* nouns, you use **il** before those beginning with most consonants* (**il pesce**), **lo** with those beginning with **gn**, **ps**, **z**, or **s** + consonant (**lo spuntino**) and **l'** with those beginning with a vowel (**l'antipasto**). With feminine* nouns, you use **la** if they start with a consonant (**la bistecca**) and **l'** if they start with a vowel (**l'aragosta**). The definite articles also change according to whether the noun is singular* or plural*.

masculine   feminine

il becomes **i** (*il pesce/i pesci*)   **la** becomes **le** (*la bistecca/le bistecche*)
lo becomes **gli** (*lo spuntino/gli spuntini*)   **l'** becomes **le** (*l'aragosta/le aragoste*)
l' becomes **gli** (*l'antipasto/gli antipasti*)

- **Volere** (to want) is another irregular verb* which you'll often come across.

(io)   **voglio** I want   (noi) **vogliamo** we want
(tu)   **vuoi** you want   (voi) **volete** you want
(lui/lei; lei) **vuole** he/she/it wants; you want (*formal*)   (loro) **vogliono** they want

Related to this verb is **vorrei** (I'd like), useful when making polite requests.

ACTIVITY 13

Match the following questions with the correct answers.

1. Vuole ordinare?
2. Cosa consiglia?
3. Vuole la carne?
4. Cosa vuole bere?

a. Le lasagne sono buone.
b. No, sono vegetariana.
c. Una birra, grazie.
d. Sì, vorrei ordinare.

ACTIVITY 14

Listen to two people ordering some food, then write down what each one orders as a first course, a main course, and a side dish.

a) 1st course _____ main course _____ side dish _____
b) 1st course _____ main course _____ side dish _____

ACTIVITIES 15 and 16 are on the recording.

Unit 2 · EATING OUT

ACTIVITY 17 is on the recording.

DIALOGUE 2.5
- Può portare il conto, per favore?
- Subito.

[…]

- Scusi, può controllare? C'è un errore nel conto.
- C'è un errore?
- Sì, ci sono due bottiglie di vino invece di una.
- Oh, scusi. Sa, c'è tanta gente.
- Non si preoccupi. Posso pagare con la carta di credito?
- Sì, certamente. Accettiamo le carte di credito.

VOCABULARY

può …? (verb potere)	can you …? (*formal*) (to be able to)
portare	to bring
il conto	bill, check
subito	right away
controllare	to check
c'è	there is
l'errore (*m*)	mistake
nel	in the
ci sono	there are
la bottiglia	bottle
invece di	instead of
scusi	I'm sorry
sa (verb sapere)	you know (*formal*) (to know)
c'è tanta gente	it's so busy (*literally* there are so many people)
non si preoccupi	don't worry
posso (verb potere)	I can (to be able to)
la carta di credito	credit card
certamente	certainly
accettiamo (verb accettare)	we accept (to accept)

> - To say 'there is' and 'there are' you use **c'è** and **ci sono**: **c'è un errore** (there's a mistake), **ci sono due bottiglie** (there are two bottles). If you want to ask a question, simply change your intonation* (and check the recording to hear how it should sound): **c'è un errore?** (is there a mistake?). If you want to use it in the negative form, just add **non**: **non ci sono errori** (there aren't any mistakes).
> - The verb* **potere** is followed by another verb in the infinitive* (**possiamo pagare** – we can pay). **potere** is conjugated as follows:
>
> SINGULAR
> (io) **posso** I can
> (tu) **puoi** you can
> (lui/lei; Lei) **può** he/she/it can; you can (*formal*)
>
> PLURAL
> (noi) **possiamo** we can
> (voi) **potete** you can
> (loro) **possono** they can

ACTIVITY 18

Match the Italian and English phrases and questions.

1. C'è un errore nel conto.
2. Possiamo ordinare?
3. Posso pagare con la carta di credito?
4. Ci sono due signore.
5. Può controllare, per favore?
6. C'è tanta gente.

a. Can I pay by credit card?
b. Can you check, please?
c. It's so busy.
d. There's a mistake in the bill.
e. Can we order?
f. There are two women.

ACTIVITY 19

Rearrange the sentences below to make a short dialogue.

No, mi dispiace.
Può portare il conto?
Posso pagare con la carta di credito?
Sì, subito.

ACTIVITIES 20 and 21 are on the recording.

Culture

Il bar is a real institution in Italy. People stop there at any time of the day for a quick drink or snack, or after a meal to have yet another coffee and meet up with friends. You can go in just for a glass of water or for the quintessentially Italian **caffè**. If you order **un caffè** you'll get an 'espresso'. If you want it with a dash of milk, you ask for **un macchiato** (**caldo** if you want the milk to be hot, or **freddo** if you want it cold). You can also have **un decaffeinato** (a decaffeinated coffee), or **un caffè lungo**, if you don't want it too strong. Otherwise, you can have **un cappuccino** and more frequently these days, **una tisana** (a herbal tea). Not many Italians drink tea in a bar but you can certainly get it. You'll need to specify if you want it with milk, otherwise you'll very likely get it **al limone** (with lemon). Another nice hot drink to have in a bar is **la cioccolata calda** (hot chocolate). In Italian bars, you very often drink and have a snack standing at the bar, but in most places you'll also find tables where you can sit at no extra charge. In posher bars where you sit down and are served by a waiter, you're charged extra since you're paying for **la consumazione al tavolo** (drinking or eating at the table).

As you may have noticed in the dialogues, Italians don't tend to use **per favore** (please), and **grazie** (thank you) as often as the British and Americans. It's just the way it is and it's not considered rude if you enter a bar and just say '**un cappuccino**'. What's important is very often the tone of your voice and the expression on your face. If you're worried about not getting it right and sounding rude, feel free to compensate by using **per favore** and **grazie** as often as you like. There isn't usually a service charge in Italian restaurants, though in tourist resorts you may find that they add 10%. However, you're always charged for **il coperto** (cover charge).

ACTIVITY 22

You went out for dinner with a friend. Both of you had a starter, a first course and a main course. Only one of you had a side dish. You shared a carafe of wine and a bottle of water. Then you had a coffee and your friend had **un liquore** (a liqueur). Read the bill and check if the waiter has filled in the correct quantities.

3	COPERTI	2,40
1	VINO – BIRRA	7,50
2	ACQUA MINERALE	4,00
3	ANTIPASTI	9,00
2	PRIMI	16,00
1	SECONDI	9,00
1	CONTORNI	4,00
2	CAFFÈ – LIQUORI	5,00
	TOTALE	**56,90 €**

ACTIVITY 23

On the recording, two women have come into a bar for a drink. Listen to their conversation with the barman and fill in the gaps.

- ● _____ macchiato.
- ■ Caldo o _____?
- ● Freddo.
- ◆ E io un _____.
- ■ _____ limone?
- ◆ No, con latte, _____ favore.
- ■ Subito.

Review 2

1. Match the Italian with its English equivalent.

1. **Un succo d'arancia.**
2. **Vorrei due tramezzini.**
3. **Cosa prendete?**
4. **Hai fame?**
5. **Non ho spiccioli.**
6. **Pago una tisana.**
7. **Una brioche e un caffè.**
8. **Quant'è?**

a. Are you hungry?
b. A croissant and a coffee.
c. I don't have any change.
d. I'm paying for a herbal tea.
e. What would you like?
f. How much is it?
g. An orange juice.
h. I'd like two sandwiches.

2. Now match the questions with the correct answers.

1. **Cosa prendi?**
2. **Hai molta fame?**
3. **Quant'è?**
4. **Volete bere qualcosa?**
5. **Hai sete?**
6. **Non ha spiccioli?**

a. Diciotto euro e cinque.
b. Io una birra e Anna un succo.
c. Una coca e un panino.
d. No, non ho spiccioli.
e. Sì, ho molta fame.
f. No, non ho sete.

3. Put the following dialogue in the right order.

Vorrei una bistecca.
Vuole ordinare?
Prendo i ravioli.
Cosa vuole bere?
E come secondo? Abbiamo carne o pesce.
I ravioli sono freschi.
Sì. Cosa consiglia come primo?
Come contorno ci sono spinaci o insalata mista.
Vino bianco e acqua gassata.
Gli spinaci.

Time to listen

4. Listen to the recording and fill in the gaps.

- Caroline _____ prendi?
- Un _____ d'arancia e un tramezzino.
- Io un _____ d'acqua e _____ caffè.
- Non _____ fame?
- No, ho _____ .

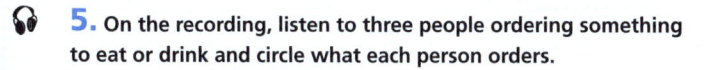

5. On the recording, listen to three people ordering something to eat or drink and circle what each person orders.

1) What does the first person order?
   a. A coffee and a croissant.
   b. Tea with milk and a croissant.
   c. A lemon tea and a croissant.
2) What does the second person order?
   a. A glass of water, a Coca-Cola® and a sandwich.
   b. An orange juice and a roll.
   c. A glass of milk and a sandwich.
3) What does the third person order?
   a. A coffee and two cappuccinos.
   b. A coffee with a dash of hot milk and a cappuccino.
   c. A croissant and two cappuccinos.

Time to talk

6. You're now going to take part in a conversation. Prepare what you want to say using the prompts and, when you're ready, do the activity on the recording.

(Say 'I'd like to order.')
– Subito signore.
(Say 'A mixed starter.')
– E come primo?
(Ask 'How's the saffron rice?')
– Molto buono.
(Say 'I'll have the rice. And for the main course what do you recommend?')
– Il pesce è fresco, la carne molto buona.
(Say 'The steak.')
– Vuole un contorno?
(Say 'No, I don't want the side dish.')
– Da bere? Acqua gassata o naturale?
(Say 'Sparkling water and red wine.')

7. Now test your progress in Unit 2. How would you say:

a. A sandwich and a Coca-Cola®, please.
b. A coffee with a dash of cold milk.
c. Tom, Liz, what are you having to drink?
d. I'm paying for one tea, three orange juices and four coffees.
e. Sorry, I don't understand. How much is it?
f. I don't have any change, I'm sorry.
g. Can you bring the bill?
h. There's a mistake in the bill. Can you check please?

You can check your answers on the recording.

Unit 3

Accommodation

In this unit you will learn how to:

- book a room in a B&B over the phone
- check in at a hotel
- find out about campsite facilities
- make complaints and requests
- count up to 1000

When listening to the recordings, make full use of the information supplied. The tone of voice is the clue to understanding whether a question is being asked or a statement made. In most cases, part of the answer to a question can be found in the question itself.

Unit 3 · ACCOMMODATION

ACTIVITY 1 is on the recording.

DIALOGUE 3.1

- Pronto? Pensione Monte Rosa.
- Buongiorno. Avete una camera per domenica notte?
- Singola o doppia?
- Doppia.
- Un attimo, controllo … Sì, abbiamo una doppia con bagno.
- Quanto costa?
- 90 euro a notte, compresa la prima colazione.
- Va bene, vorrei prenotare per una notte. Il cognome è Kapur.
- Come si scrive, scusi?
- K, a, p, u, r.

VOCABULARY

pronto?	hello? (*on the phone*)
la pensione	B&B, guest house
la camera	(bed)room
per	for
domenica notte	Sunday night
singolo/-a	single
doppio/-a	double
un attimo	one moment (please)
con bagno	with bathroom
quanto costa?	how much is it?
a notte	per night
compreso/-a	including (*also* included)
la (prima) colazione	breakfast
va bene	that's fine
prenotare	to book
il cognome	surname, last name
come si scrive?	how do you spell it? (*literally* how is it written?)

Unit 3 · ACCOMMODATION

> • Here are some more numbers, from 21 to 29 and then 30, 40, etc. up to 90.
> You'll have the opportunity to practise their pronunciation on the recording.
>
> | | | | |
> |---|---|---|---|
> | 21 **ventuno** | 25 **venticinque** | 29 **ventinove** | 60 **sessanta** |
> | 22 **ventidue** | 26 **ventisei** | 30 **trenta** | 70 **settanta** |
> | 23 **ventitré** | 27 **ventisette** | 40 **quaranta** | 80 **ottanta** |
> | 24 **ventiquattro** | 28 **ventotto** | 50 **cinquanta** | 90 **novanta** |
>
> • In the dialogue, you heard **domenica** which means 'Sunday'. The others days of the week are:
>
> | | | | |
> |---|---|---|---|
> | **lunedì** | Monday | **giovedì** | Thursday |
> | **martedì** | Tuesday | **venerdì** | Friday |
> | **mercoledì** | Wednesday | **sabato** | Saturday |
>
> They're all masculine* apart from **la domenica**, which is feminine*.
>
> • You can practise how to pronounce the letters of the alphabet on the recording.

ACTIVITY 2

Reorder the following five strings of words to create five sentences.

una/singola/camera/ha?
costa/notte/quanto/a?
scrive/come/scusi/si?
colazione/compresa/è/la.
camera/prenotare/vorrei/una.

ACTIVITY 3

Listen to the recording and choose true or false for each statement below.

1. The woman wants a double room   TRUE/FALSE
2. She wants the room for Monday night.   TRUE/FALSE
3. The room costs 40 euros per night.   TRUE/FALSE
4. The receptionist knows how to spell 'Scott'.   TRUE/FALSE

ACTIVITIES 4 and 5 are on the recording.

Unit 3 · ACCOMMODATION

ACTIVITY 6 is on the recording.

DIALOGUE 3.2
- Buonasera.
- Buonasera. Sono Timothy Evans. Ho una stanza prenotata per stanotte.
- Vediamo … Una camera singola con bagno?
- Sì.
- Posso avere un documento?
- Ecco il mio passaporto.
- Grazie. La sua è la camera numero settantanove. Questa è la sua chiave.

VOCABULARY

la stanza	room
prenotato/-a	booked
stanotte	tonight
vediamo (verb vedere)	let's see (to see)
il documento	identification (*literally* document)
mio/-a	my
il passaporto	passport
il numero	number
questo/-a	this, this one
suo/-a	your (*formal*)
la chiave	key

- The word for 'this' (**questo/-a**) behaves exactly like all other adjectives* ending in **-o**. So you have **quest*i* documenti/quest*e* camere**.
- To indicate *who* owns *what* (or possession), you use possessive adjectives*. In Italian, the words for 'my', 'your', etc. change like all adjectives. Unlike English, these possessive adjectives agree* with 'the *what*' rather than 'the *who*' so that 'her passport' is *il suo* **passaporto** in Italian. **Passaporto** is a masculine* noun* which requires a matching masculine possessive adjective. Possessives are usually preceded by the definite article* **il**, **la**, **i**, **le**, etc. Here's how it works:
il **passaporto di Mr Scott/Mrs Kapur** (Mr Scott's/Mrs Kapur's passport) →
il suo **passaporto** (his/her passport)

!

la camera *di* Timothy/Anna (Timothy's/Anna's room) →
la *sua* camera (his/her room)
i documenti *di* Mr Scott/Mrs Kapur (Mr Scott's/Mrs Kapur's documents) →
i *suoi* documenti (his/her documents)
le chiavi *di* Timothy/Anna (Timothy's/Anna's keys) →
le *sue* chiavi (his/her keys)

The table below lists all the possible forms of Italian possessive adjectives.

		masculine	feminine		masculine	feminine
my	singular	**il mio**	**la mia**	plural	**i miei**	**le mie**
your (*informal*)		**il tuo**	**la tua**		**i tuoi**	**le tue**
his/her/its		**il suo**	**la sua**		**i suoi**	**le sue**
your (*formal*)		**il suo**	**la sua**		**i suoi**	**le sue**
our		**il nostro**	**la nostra**		**i nostri**	**le nostre**
your		**il vostro**	**la vostra**		**i vostri**	**le vostre**
their		**il loro**	**la loro**		**i loro**	**le loro**

ACTIVITY 7

Match the questions and answers.

1. Ha una camera prenotata?
2. Posso avere un documento?
3. C'è il bagno in camera?
4. Questa è la mia chiave?

a. Ecco i nostri passaporti.
b. No, questa qui è la sua chiave.
c. Sì, una doppia.
d. Sì, è una doppia con bagno.

ACTIVITY 8

Listen to dialogue 3.2 again and choose true or false for the following:

1. Mr Evans has a room booked. TRUE/FALSE
2. It's a double room. TRUE/FALSE
3. Mr Evans gives the receptionist his driving licence. TRUE/FALSE
4. Mr Evans is in room number 97. TRUE/FALSE

ACTIVITIES 9 and 10 are on the recording.

Unit 3 · ACCOMMODATION

ACTIVITY 11 is on the recording.

DIALOGUE 3.3
- Buongiorno. Cerchiamo un campeggio qui vicino.
- Il camping 'Il gabbiano' è appena fuori città ed è proprio sul mare.
- Quanto costa?
- La piazzola per la tenda costa 60 euro a notte.
- Un po' cara. Il campeggio è ben attrezzato?
- Sì. Ci sono molti gabinetti e molte docce, anche per i disabili. C'è il mini-market, l'infermeria e il deposito bagagli.
- Qual è l'indirizzo?
- Via Aurelia 600, Bibbiena. E il numero di telefono è 0577/80 02 63.
- Grazie.
- Prego.

VOCABULARY

cerchiamo (verb cercare)	we're looking for (to look for)
il campeggio/il camping	campsite, campground
qui vicino	nearby
il gabbiano	seagull
appena	just
fuori	outside
la città	town
proprio	right
sul mare	by the sea
la piazzola	pitch, site
la tenda	tent
un po'	a bit
caro/-a	expensive
ben attrezzato/-a	well equipped
molti/-e	lots of, many
il gabinetto	toilet
la doccia/-ce	shower
anche	also
i disabili	the disabled
il mini-market	mini-market
l'infermeria (f)	first-aid room

VOCABULARY

il deposito bagagli	left luggage facility
qual è l'indirizzo?	what's the address?
la via	road
il numero di telefono	telephone number
prego	you're welcome

(!)

- There's no standard way of saying telephone numbers in Italian. You can say the numbers one after the other, two by two or three at a time. You'll need the area code, **il prefisso**, even for local calls.
- Here are some more numbers:

100 **cento**	500 **cinquecento**	900 **novecento**
200 **duecento**	600 **seicento**	1000 **mille**
300 **trecento**	700 **settecento**	2000 **duemila**
400 **quattrocento**	800 **ottocento**	

ACTIVITY 12

Match the English and Italian phrases below.

1. I'm looking for a campsite by the sea.
2. How much is the pitch per night?
3. Is there a left luggage facility?
4. What's the address?
5. It's a bit expensive.

a. Quanto costa la piazzola a notte?
b. È un po' caro.
c. Qual è l'indirizzo?
d. C'è un deposito bagagli?
e. Cerco un campeggio sul mare.

ACTIVITY 13

Say the following telephone numbers. You can check your pronunciation on the recording. The last one is for a mobile phone, **un cellulare**.

031/44 52 60   02/63 71 59   349/99 57 21 5

ACTIVITIES 14 and 15 are on the recording.

Unit 3 · ACCOMMODATION

ACTIVITY 16 is on the recording.

DIALOGUE 3.4
- Pronto? Reception.
- Buonasera. Chiamo dalla camera settantanove, al terzo piano.
- Desidera?
- C'è un problema. La luce nel bagno non funziona. E non riesco a regolare l'aria condizionata.
- Mando subito qualcuno a controllare. Altro?
- Posso avere un altro cuscino per favore?
- Certamente.

VOCABULARY

chiamo (verb chiamare)	I'm calling (to call)
dalla	from the
al terzo piano	on the third floor
desidera?	can I help you?
il problema	problem
la luce	light
funziona (verb funzionare)	it works (to work, *literally* to function)
non riesco a (verb riuscire)	I can't (to be able to, to succeed)
regolare	to regulate
l'aria condizionata (f)	air conditioning
mando (verb mandare)	I'll send (to send)
qualcuno	someone
altro?	anything else?
un altro/un'altra	another, an extra (*also* a different one)
il cuscino	pillow

!

Here's a list of ordinal numbers* (first, second, third etc.) from 1st to 10th. Like all adjectives*, they change their endings* if the nouns* they refer to are feminine* or plural*. So you'll find **il primo piano** but **la prima colazione**.
1st **primo/-a**   2nd **secondo/-a**   3rd **terzo/-a**   4th **quarto/-a**
5th **quinto/-a**   6th **sesto/-a**   7th **settimo/-a**   8th **ottavo/-a**
9th **nono/-a**   10th **decimo/-a**
You'll have the opportunity to practise them on the recording.

Unit 3 · ACCOMMODATION

> • In the units so far, you'll have come across short words (called prepositions*) like **a**, **di**, **in**, and **per**. Other common prepositions are **da** (from, at), **con** (with), **su** (on), **tra** or **fra** (between *or* in, when referring to time – **tra/fra due giorni** – in 2 days' time). These can be followed by a noun: *a Roma* (in Rome), *in vacanza* (on holiday). They can however also precede a verb but they won't be translated literally: **qualcosa** *da bere* (something to drink), **non riesco** *a regolare* l'aria condizionata (I can't regulate the air conditioning), **mando qualcuno** *a controllare* (I'll send someone to check).
>
> When followed by a noun, some prepositions merge with the definite article*. So you can have **dalla** (**dalla camera 79** = from room 79), **nel** (**nel conto** = in the bill), **al** (**al terzo piano** = on the third floor), **sul** (**sul mare** = by the sea), etc. Don't worry about getting them exactly right as they're quite complicated. It's enough that you recognize them when you come across them.

ACTIVITY 17

Match the English with the Italian.

1. We have a problem.
2. The light in our room doesn't work.
3. Can you send someone to check?
4. I'd like an extra pillow.

a. Può mandare qualcuno a controllare?
b. Abbiamo un problema.
c. Vorrei un altro cuscino.
d. La luce nella nostra camera non funziona.

ACTIVITY 18

Fill in the gaps to complete the following complaints and requests.

La TV non _____.

Non _____ a regolare l'aria condizionata.

Può _____ qualcuno a controllare?

Vorrei un' _____ stanza.

ACTIVITIES 19 and 20 are on the recording.

Culture

When looking for accommodation, you have at least two main options: **l'hotel** (*m*), also known as **l'albergo** (*m*), or **la pensione** which is the equivalent of a B&B or guest house. In a **pensione**, you can book **la camera e la prima colazione** only (room and breakfast), but you can also go for **la pensione completa** (full board) or **la mezza pensione** (half board) so it's quite flexible.

Other options are **l'ostello della gioventù** (youth hostel) and **il campeggio** or **il camping** (campsite). Good guide books or **il centro informazioni turistiche** (tourist office) have lists with details of hotel categories, star ratings, facilities and prices. The price of a room can vary drastically depending on the time of year: **l'alta stagione** (high season), **la mezza stagione** (mid-season) and **la bassa stagione** (low season).

Whichever option you decide on, be sure to book in advance if you're planning to visit popular holiday resorts during the high season. An expression you really don't want to hear is **'siamo al completo'** (we're full).

When you check in at a hotel or **pensione**, you'll be asked for some form of ID such as **il passaporto** (passport), so your details can be registered. You'll get it back right away or they may keep it until you check out, which could be a problem if you need identification to change travellers' cheques, for example, during your stay.

In Italy people are issued with **la carta d'identità** (identity card). This gives your name, your profession and your address as well as details about your height, hair colour etc. and the obligatory photo (terrible, of course). Italians can use it as an alternative to a passport to travel abroad within the EU. In Italy it's compulsory to carry some form of ID with you at all times. This can be an identity card, or a passport if you're a foreigner. It's more and more common to be stopped by police and asked for **'documenti'** on trains and in the street. It's very often a routine procedure and nothing to worry about (as long as you've got nothing to hide!). If you're stopped and you don't have any ID on you, you may well be asked to go to the police station to prove that your papers are in order.

ACTIVITY 21

> LINEA ESTERNA – OUTSIDE LINE 0
> RECEPTION 9
> SVEGLIA – ALARM SET
> 191 + HH/MM ATTIVATA/ ALARM ON
> 180 DISATTIVATA/ALARM OFF

The above **depliant** (leaflet) in your hotel room illustrates how to set **la sveglia** (the phone alarm) but you can't get it to work. You call reception for help. Try and complete the following dialogue. Once you've filled in as many gaps as you can, listen to the full conversation on the recording and fill in any remaining blanks.

- Pronto? Reception. _____?
- _____ dalla camera 39. Ho _____ _____. Non _____ _____ attivare la sveglia.
- Ha il depliant? Ha capito come funziona?
- Sì, _____ capito. Ma _____ funziona.
- Il _____ è 181?
- Ah, no. C'è un _____ sul depliant. Il numero qui è 191!

Review 3

1. Match the English questions with their Italian equivalents.

1. Have you got a double room?
2. Can I have my passport?
3. How much is it per night?
4. Is breakfast included?
5. What's the address?
6. Is there a campsite nearby?
7. How do you spell 'Il gabbiano'?

a. Qual è l'indirizzo?
b. Posso avere il mio passaporto
c. Avete una camera doppia?
d. C'è un campeggio qui vicino?
e. Quanto costa a notte?
f. Come si scrive 'Il gabbiano'?
g. La prima colazione è compresa?

2. And now match the Italian with the English.

1. Vuole prenotare una camera?
2. La pensione è sul mare.
3. Siamo al completo, mi dispiace.
4. Ha il nostro indirizzo?
5. La camera singola non ha il bagno.

a. Have you got our address?
b. I'm sorry, we're full.
c. Do you want to book a room?
d. The single room hasn't got a bathroom.
e. The B&B is by the sea.

3. Someone's looking for a B&B and stops at the tourist office to make some enquiries. Fill in the gaps.

– Buongiorno. Cerco _____ pensione qui _____ .
– _____ pensione Monte Rosa _____ proprio qui vicino.
– Quanto _____ una camera doppia?
– Non è cara, 70 euro a notte.
– Qual è l' _____ ?
– Via Roma 26.
– Grazie.
– _____ .

Time to listen

4. Simona Vitti arrives at a hotel with a friend. On the recording, listen to her conversation at reception and mark whether the following statements are true or false.

1. They don't have a room booked. TRUE/FALSE
2. They have a double room booked. TRUE/FALSE
3. They have a double room without bathroom. TRUE/FALSE
4. They have the room for three nights. TRUE/FALSE
5. They give the receptionist their passports. TRUE/FALSE
6. They're in room number 132. TRUE/FALSE

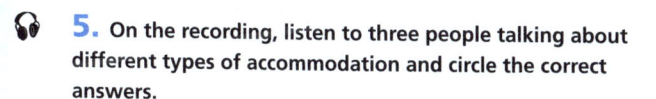

5. On the recording, listen to three people talking about different types of accommodation and circle the correct answers.

1) What does he say?
   a. He says he'd like to book a room for two nights.
   b. He asks if they have a single room for tonight.
   c. He asks where there's a B&B.
2) What does she ask?
   a. She asks how much a pitch at the campsite 'Il gabbiano' is.
   b. She asks where the B&B 'Il gabbiano' is.
   c. She asks where the campsite 'Il gabbiano' is.
3) What does he want?
   a. He'd like to book for another night.
   b. He asks if they have a room for two nights.
   c. He'd like to book a double room.

Unit 3 · ACCOMMODATION

Time to talk

6. You're now going to take part in a conversation. Prepare what you are going to say using the prompts. Then, when you're ready, do the activity on the recording.

– Buongiorno.
(Ask 'Is there a campsite nearby?')
– Sì. Ci sono due campeggi. Uno è sul mare, uno no.
(Say 'We want the campsite by the sea.')
– Allora è il camping 'Il gabbiano'.
(Ask 'How much is the pitch per night?')
– Una piazzola costa 60 euro a notte.
(Ask 'Is the campsite well equipped?')
– Sì, è molto ben attrezzato. Ci sono molti gabinetti e molte docce, c'è il mini-market e l'infermeria.
(Ask 'Is there a bar?')
– Il bar è molto vicino al campeggio.
(Ask 'What's the address?')
– Via del Mare 699.

7. Now test your progress in Unit 3. How would you say:

a. Have you got two double rooms? (*formal*)
b. How much are they?
c. Is breakfast included?
d. Here's my passport.
e. I'm calling from room 53.
f. Can you send someone to check? (*formal*)
g. I can't regulate the air conditioning.
h. The TV doesn't work.
i. Can I have another pillow, please?

You can check your answers on the recording.

Unit 4

Getting around

In this unit you will learn how to:
- catch a person's attention
- ask for directions
- ask about public transport
- ask the time and answer the same question

If you haven't quite got all the words you need or you feel unsure about your ability to form complete, correct sentences, don't be put off. Make the most of the words you do know, use facial expressions and gestures, draw pictures. There's more to communication than just knowing the right words and using perfect grammar.

Unit 4 · GETTING AROUND

🎧 ACTIVITY 1 is on the recording.

DIALOGUE 4.1

- Scusi, per andare al museo archeologico?
- Il museo è in piazza Raffaello.
- Come ci arrivo?
- Lei va dritto e all'incrocio gira a destra. Poi prosegue fino alla piazza. Quella è piazza Raffaello. Il museo è a sinistra, di fronte alla chiesa.
- Vado dritto, poi all'incrocio giro a destra.
- Esatto.
- È lontano da qui? Quanto ci vuole a piedi?
- Non è lontano, a piedi sono dieci minuti.

VOCABULARY

il museo	museum
archeologico/-a	archaeological
in	in
la piazza	square
come ci arrivo?	how do I get there?
va/vado (verb andare)	you (*formal*) go/I go (to go)
dritto	straight on
l'incrocio (*m*)	crossroads
gira a destra (verb girare)	turn right (*formal*) (to turn)
poi	then
prosegue (verb proseguire)	keep going (*formal*) (to keep going)
fino alla piazza	up to the square
quello/-a	that, that one
a sinistra	on the left
di fronte a	opposite
la chiesa	church
esatto/-a	correct
lontano/-a	far
da qui	from here
quanto ci vuole a piedi?	how long does it take to walk there?
il minuto	minute

- To catch someone's attention and ask for directions or other information, you say **scusi**, (excuse me) or **scusa** (*informal*), and **scusate** if you're addressing more than one person (both formally and informally). The same phrases are also used to apologize so, in other contexts, they're translated by 'I'm sorry'.
- In the dialogue, you'll have heard **andare**, meaning 'to go'. The verb is conjugated* in the table below. You can practise your pronunciation on the recording while working through it.

(io)	**vado** I go		(noi)	**andiamo** we go
(tu)	**vai** you go		(voi)	**andate** you go
(lui/lei; lei)	**va** he/she/it goes; you go (*formal*)		(loro)	**vanno** they go

ACTIVITY 2

Match the questions with the appropriate answers.

1. Scusi, per andare al museo?
2. Quanto ci vuole?
3. È lontano?
4. All'incrocio giro a sinistra?

a. A piedi sono cinque minuti.
b. Lei gira a destra e poi a sinistra.
c. Esatto, a sinistra.
d. No, non è lontano.

ACTIVITY 3

Look at the map and choose true or false for the directions to the church.

1. Andate dritto.
   TRUE/FALSE
2. Girate a destra.
   TRUE/FALSE
3. Proseguite fino alla piazza.
   TRUE/FALSE
4. La chiesa è a sinistra, di fronte all'albergo Milano.
   TRUE/FALSE

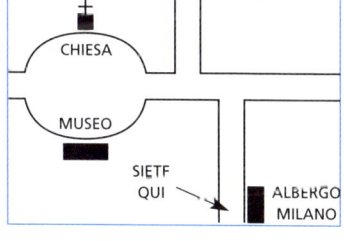

ACTIVITIES 4 and 5 are on the recording.

ACTIVITY 6 is on the recording.

DIALOGUE 4.2

- Scusa, quale linea di metropolitana prendo per andare alla stazione?
- La linea blu va alla stazione. Ma da qui si fa prima con l'autobus.
- Quale autobus va alla stazione?
- Il numero quattro porta proprio davanti alla stazione.
- Qual è la fermata?
- È là, di fronte alla farmacia.
- Dove compro il biglietto dell'autobus?
- Dal giornalaio. Ma anche l'autista dell'autobus vende i biglietti.
- E, scusa, a quale fermata devo scendere?
- Scendi all'ultima fermata.

VOCABULARY

quale, qual	which, what
la linea	line
la metropolitana	underground, subway
prendo (verb prendere)	I take (to take)
la stazione	station
blu	blue
si fa prima	it's quicker
l'autobus (m)	bus
porta (verb portare)	it takes you (to take) (*said of a bus, etc.*)
davanti a	in front of; opposite
la fermata	bus stop
là/lì	there
di fronte a	in front of; opposite
la farmacia	chemist's, pharmacy
compro (verb comprare)	I buy (to buy)
il biglietto	ticket
dal giornalaio	at the newsagent's
l'autista (m/f)	driver
vende (verb vendere)	he/she sells (to sell)
scendi (verb scendere)	get off (*informal*) (to get off)
ultimo/-a	last (one)

- The Italian equivalent of 'which' is **quale**: *which bus do I take?* ***quale autobus prendo?*** (or **quali** if it's more than one). You can also use **quale** to ask 'which one': *which one is the bus stop for piazza Roma?* ***qual è la fermata per piazza Roma?*** (note how **quale** is shortened to **qual** here, with no apostrophe) or *which one do you want?* ***quale vuoi?***
- In the dialogue, you heard **a quale fermata devo scendere?** (*which stop do I get off at?*). In Italian, the preposition* (at, from, with, etc.) always goes at the beginning of the question whereas it can often appear at the end in English.
- In the previous unit you also came across **quale** as an equivalent of **what**: ***qual è l'indirizzo?*** (*what's the address?*)

ACTIVITY 7

Match the English questions with their Italian equivalents.

1. Where can I buy the ticket?
2. Where's the bus stop?
3. Does the 4 take you to the station?
4. Which stop do I get off at?
5. How do I get to the square?
6. Which bus do I take?
7. Which is the line for the museum?

a. Dov'è la fermata dell'autobus?
b. A quale fermata scendo?
c. Quale autobus prendo?
d. Dove compro il biglietto?
e. Il quattro porta alla stazione?
f. Qual è la linea per il museo?
g. Come arrivo alla piazza?

ACTIVITY 8

Listen to the conversation on the recording and answer the questions below in English.

1. Is it far to walk to the station?
2. Can they take a bus?
3. Which bus goes to the station?
4. Where's the bus stop?

ACTIVITIES 9 and 10 are on the recording.

ACTIVITY 11 is on the recording.

DIALOGUE 4.3

- Scusi, per andare a Firenze?
- Ha sbagliato strada. L'autostrada per Firenze è dall'altra parte.
- Come ci arrivo?
- Deve tornare indietro …
- Può parlare più lentamente, per favore?
- Sì, scusi. Deve tornare indietro verso il paese. Alla rotonda deve prendere la prima a destra.
- Alla rotonda devo prendere la prima a destra?
- Sì, poi deve proseguire dritto e girare quando vede il cartello per l'autostrada. Ha capito?
- Spero di sì. Grazie mille.

VOCABULARY

per andare a … ?	how do I get to …? (*literally* to go to)
Firenze	Florence
ha sbagliato strada	you're (*formal*) on the wrong road
l'autostrada (*f*)	motorway, freeway
dall'altra parte	on the other side
deve/devo (verb dovere)	you must (*formal*)/I must (to have to)
tornare indietro	to go back
parlare	to speak, talk
più	more
lentamente	slowly
verso	towards
il paese	village
la rotonda	roundabout, traffic circle
quando	when
il cartello	sign
spero di sì	I hope so
grazie mille	thanks very much

The verb* **dovere** crops up a lot in the last dialogue. It is always followed by another verb in the infinitive*: ***deve tornare* indietro** (you must turn back). Study the verb table. You can practise your pronunciation on the recording.

(io)	**devo** I must	(noi)	**dobbiamo** we must
(tu)	**devi** you must	(voi)	**dovete** you must
(lui/lei; lei)	**deve** he/she/it must; you must (*formal*)	(loro)	**devono** they must

ACTIVITY 12

Someone's asking how to get to the motorway to Rome. Fill in the gaps to complete the conversation.

- Scusi, per _____ _____ Roma.
- _____ andare dritto, poi al _____ girare _____ destra per l'autostrada.
- Dove _____ girare?
- Deve _____ al semaforo.
- C'è un _____ ?
- Sì, c'è un cartello.

ACTIVITY 13

Listen to dialogue 4.3 again and circle the correct answers.

1) Where does he want to go?
   a. He wants to go to the the station.
   b. He wants to go to Florence.
   c. He wants to go to the village.

2) Is he on the right road?
   a. He's on the right road.
   b. He's on the wrong road.
   c. The passer-by doesn't know.

3) What does he have to do?
   a. He has to turn back.
   b. He has to turn left.
   c. He has to keep going straight on.

ACTIVITIES 14 and 15 are on the recording.

ACTIVITY 16 is on the recording.

DIALOGUE 4.4

- Scusi, è questo il treno per l'aeroporto?
- No, questo va a Roma. Il treno per l'aeroporto è al binario otto.
- A che ora parte?
- Parte alle nove e dieci.
- È in orario?
- È in ritardo di cinque minuti.
- A che ora arriva all'aeroporto?
- Impiega circa un'ora. Arriva verso le dieci e un quarto.
- E, scusi, che ore sono?
- Sono le nove meno cinque.
- Grazie mille.

VOCABULARY

il treno	train
l'aeroporto (*m*)	airport
il binario	platform
a che ora … ?	(at) what time …?
parte (verb partire)	leaves (to leave)
alle nove e dieci	at ten (minutes) past nine
in orario	on time
in ritardo	late
impiega (verb impiegare)	takes (to take) (*speaking of time*)
circa	about
l'ora (*f*)	hour
verso	around
le dieci e un quarto	a quarter past ten
che ore sono?	what time is it?
le nove meno cinque	five (minutes) to nine

- As you've seen in the dialogue, to ask 'what time is it?', you use **che ore sono?** and to say '(at) what time … ?' you use **a che ora … ?**
Here are the most useful models for saying what time it is in Italian:
it's nine/ten/eleven o'clock   **sono le nove/le dieci/le undici**

!

The exceptions are:
it's one o'clock **è l'una**
it's midday/midnight **è mezzogiorno/mezzanotte**
To say:
it's five past/after nine **sono le nove e cinque**
it's a quarter past/after nine **sono le nove e un quarto**
it's half-nine **sono le nove e mezzo**
To say:
it's twenty to ten **sono le dieci meno venti** (**meno** = 'minus')
it's a quarter to ten **sono le dieci meno un quarto**

Italians don't use am and pm. To specify which it is, they say **le nove di mattina** (nine in the morning) for 9 am and **le nove di sera** (nine in the evening) for 9 pm; **le tre di mattina** for 3 am and **le tre di pomeriggio** (3 in the afternoon) for 3 pm.
In more formal contexts (timetables, written language), the 24-hour clock is used:
il treno arriva alle ventuno e trenta (21:30)
la partenza (departure) **è alle diciassette e cinquanta** (17:50)
l'arrivo (arrival) **è alle ventiquattro e zero cinque** (00:05)

ACTIVITY 17

Look at the time on the right and answer the questions in Italian.

What time is it?	14:20
When does the film start?	21:30 (to start = cominciare)
At what time do you arrive?	16:00
What time does the bus leave at?	10:40

ACTIVITY 18

Listen to the train announcements on the recording and choose true or false.

1. The train to Venice is arriving at platform 6. T/F
2. The train to Florence is arriving at platform 2. T/F
3. The 17:50 train is 25 minutes late. T/F
4. The train to Bologna leaves from platform 7 instead of platform 2. T/F

ACTIVITIES 19 and 20 are on the recording.

Culture

Italian people usually try to help if you stop them to ask for information or directions. This doesn't automatically mean that they're always helpful, especially if you can't understand what they're saying and vice versa. Keep on trying to use your Italian to get the message across and don't be afraid to use phrases like:

Come, scusi? (Pardon?)
Non ho capito. (I don't understand.)
Può parlare più lentamente? (Could you speak more slowly?)
Può ripetere? (Could you say that again please?)

The language barrier can often be overcome through body language. Italians use their hands a lot while speaking and, in the context of giving directions, this can be especially useful. So if you're really stuck for words, don't be shy and just do as they do.

When walking around town and asking for directions, what might initially seem obscure are the distances given in metres. So, for instance, when you ask **È lontana piazza Navona?** (Is piazza Navona far?), be prepared for answers like **Duecento metri** (200 metres, i.e. just over 200 yards) or **È a cinquecento metri**. (It's 500 metres away, i.e. just over 500 yards).

ACTIVITY 21

You're at a restaurant and you ask the waiter for directions to the toilet. When an English-speaking friend of yours asks you the same question, are you able to tell her the way?

You: Scusi, dov'è la toilette?
Waiter: Al primo piano, a sinistra.
You: Non ho capito. Può ripetere, per favore?
Waiter: Al primo piano, a sinistra.
You: Grazie.
Your friend: Where's the toilet?
You: The toilet is _____.

ACTIVITY 22

Someone's asking where the telephone is. Fill in the gaps.

Scusi, _____ inglese?
_____, mi dispiace.
C'è _____ telefono?
In fondo _____ destra.

ACTIVITY 23

Simona asks a passer-by how to get to corso Verdi. Look at the map. From the directions given on the recording, can you work out where she is now?

a. She's in piazza Raffaello.
b. She's at the station.
c. She's in corso Verdi.
d. She's at the church of S. Paolo.

Review 4

1. Match the English with the Italian.

1. Excuse me, how do I get to the museum?
2. Is it far to walk from here?
3. Which bus goes to the station?
4. Does the blue line go to the church of S. Paolo?
5. Which stop do I get off at for the museum?
6. Thank you very much.

a. **A quale fermata scendo per il museo?**
b. **Grazie mille.**
c. **Scusi, per andare al museo?**
d. **Quale autobus va alla stazione?**
e. **La linea blu va alla chiesa di San Paolo?**
f. **È lontano da qui a piedi?**

2. Now match the questions with the correct answers.

1. **Scusi, è questo il treno per l'aeroporto?**
2. **Da che binario parte il treno per Firenze?**
3. **A che ora parte il treno per Bologna?**
4. **A che ora arriva all'aeroporto?**
5. **Scusi, che ore sono?**
6. **Dov'è la toilette?**

a. In fondo a sinistra.
b. Dal binario cinque.
c. No, questo treno va a Pisa.
d. È mezzogiorno e dieci.
e. Arriva alle sette e quarantotto.
f. Parte alle diciotto.

3. Someone is asking for directions. Fill in the gaps.

– Scusi, c'è un autobus o una _____ per andare in corso Italia?
– La metropolitana porta proprio lì.
– _____ linea devo _____ ?
– La _____ rossa.
– _____ _____ fermata devo scendere?
– Corso Italia.

Time to listen

4. **Listen to the recording where someone is giving directions to the pharmacy and circle the correct answers.**

1) Is there a pharmacy nearby?
   a. There's no pharmacy nearby.
   b. There's one in the piazza Garibaldi.
   c. There's one in the via Garibaldi.
2) How far is it?
   a. It's ten minutes from here.
   b. It's five hundred metres from here.
   c. It's a kilometre from here.
3) How do you get there?
   a. You turn left at the traffic lights.
   b. You go straight on at the traffic lights, then turn right.
   c. You turn right and then immediately left.
4) Where is the pharmacy exactly?
   a. It's on the right, opposite the newsagent's.
   b. It's on the right, next to the newsagent's.
   c. It's on the left, opposite the church.

5. **Listen to the short conversations on the recording and mark the statements below true or false.**

1. It's twenty-five past five.	TRUE/FALSE
2. He leaves at half past five.	TRUE/FALSE
3. He arrives at half past eight.	TRUE/FALSE
4. She must be at the airport at two o'clock.	TRUE/FALSE
5. The plane leaves at 16:45.	TRUE/FALSE
6. It takes two hours to get to London.	TRUE/FALSE

Unit 4 · GETTING AROUND

Time to talk

6. You're now going to take part in a conversation. Prepare what you are going to say using the prompts. Then, when you're ready, do the activity on the recording.

(Ask 'Excuse me, how do I get to the underground?')
– Deve andare dritto fino al semaforo e poi girare a sinistra.
(Ask 'Is it far?')
– Venti minuti a piedi.
(Say 'I have to go to via Verdi. Can I take a bus?')
– Sì, ci sono molti autobus per via Verdi. Il tre, il venti e il ventotto.
(Ask 'Where's the bus stop?')
– La fermata dell'autobus è quella lì.
(Ask 'Can I buy the ticket on the bus?')
– Sì, oppure dal giornalaio di fronte alla fermata.
(Say 'Pardon? Could you repeat that, please?')
– L'autista vende i biglietti oppure il giornalaio davanti alla fermata.

7. Now test your progress in Unit 4. How would you say:

a. Excuse me, how do I get to the station?
b. Could you speak more slowly please?
c. Do I turn right or left at the traffic lights?
d. Is it far to walk to the museum?
e. Excuse me, which underground line do I take to go to the archeological museum?
f. Is this the train for the airport?
g. Which platform does the train to Pisa leave from?
h. At what time does the train to Florence leave?
i. Excuse me, what time is it?
j. It's ten past eleven.

You can check your answers on the recording.

Unit 5

Shopping

In this unit you will learn how to:

- shop for food
- buy stamps, postcards and other items
- buy a present
- shop for clothes

The key to successful language learning is building on what you already know. 'Recycle' as much as possible and add new items of vocabulary as you go along. Practise putting them into sentences to fix them in your mind and at the same time reinforce what you already know.

ACTIVITY 1 is on the recording.

DIALOGUE 5.1

- Dica.
- Un po' di prosciutto crudo, un etto. E un pezzetto di parmigiano.
- Così va bene?
- No, è troppo. Un po' di meno.
  Poi mezzo chilo di panini e un pezzo di focaccia.
- Questa è abbastanza?
- No, un po' di più per favore.
- Altro?
- Delle olive e prendo due litri di latte scremato.
- Altro?
- No, basta così.

VOCABULARY

dica	can I help you? (*literally* tell me)
un po' di	a bit of, some
il prosciutto	ham
crudo/-a	cured
l'etto (*m*)	100 grams
il pezzetto	small piece
il parmigiano	parmesan cheese
troppo	too much; *also* too
un po' di meno	a bit less
mezzo/-a	half
il chilo	kilo
il pezzo	piece
abbastanza	enough
un po' di più	a bit more
altro?	anything else?
delle	some
l'oliva (*f*)	olive
il litro	litre
scremato/-a	skimmed
basta così	that's all

Unit 5 · SHOPPING

> • **Delle olive** means 'some olives'. To translate 'some', use **del** (or **dello** and **dell'**) with a masculine* singular* noun*, and **della** (or **dell'**) with a feminine* one. With plural* nouns, use **dei** (or **degli**) for masculine and **delle** for feminine:
> I'd like some milk = **vorrei del latte**
> some focaccia = **della focaccia** – some water = **dell'acqua**
> some rolls = **dei panini** – some spinach = **degli spinaci**
> (Remember that **del/della/dei/delle** can also mean 'of the'.)
> 'Some …' can also be translated by **un po' di …**:
> some milk/focaccia/rolls/olives = **un po' di latte/focaccia/panini/olive**.
> To say 'a bit more', use **un po' di più** and for 'a bit less', say **un po' di meno**.
> • On price tags for ham or cheese (**il formaggio**), you might see **hg**. referring to the weight. It stands for **ettogrammo**, usually shortened to **etto** (100g).

ACTIVITY 2

Look at Anna's shopping list and complete her conversation with the shop assistant.

– Dica.
– _____ di _____ e _____ di _____.
– Altro?
– _____ _____ e _____ _____.
– Altro?
– No, basta così.

> 2 hg prosciutto crudo
> 1 hg parmigiano
> ½ kg panini
> 1 l latte

ACTIVITY 3

Roberto's cooking dinner but hasn't got all the ingredients. On the recording, he says what he needs. Listen and write down the amounts.

le pere   l'uva   l'olio   i funghi   gli zucchini   il formaggio   il pane

_____   _____   _____   _____   _____   _____   _____

ACTIVITIES 4 and 5 are on the recording.

Unit 5 · SHOPPING

ACTIVITY 6 is on the recording.

DIALOGUE 5.2

- Un pacchetto di fazzolettini e dei chewing-gum. Quanto costano le cartoline?
- Cinquanta centesimi l'una.
- Ne prendo quattro. Ha francobolli?
- Sì.
- Due per la Gran Bretagna e due per gli Stati Uniti.
- Ecco i francobolli. In tutto sono quattro euro e quindici.
- Ha dei giornali stranieri?
- No, non vendiamo giornali. Può provare all'edicola della stazione.
- Grazie

VOCABULARY

il pacchetto	packet
il fazzolettino	tissue
dei chewing-gum (*plural*)	some chewing gum
quanto costano?	how much are they?
la cartolina	postcard
l'uno/l'una	each
ne	of them
il francobollo	stamp
la Gran Bretagna	Great Britain
gli Stati Uniti	United States
in tutto	in total
il giornale	newspaper, magazine
straniero/-a	foreign
provare	to try
l'edicola (*f*)	news-stand

The word **ne** means 'of them'. **ne prendo quattro** (I'll take four of them).
The word **né** (same pronunciation) however means 'neither'.
non hanno né francobolli né giornali. (they have *neither* stamps *nor* papers.)

ACTIVITY 7

Match the following English statements and questions with the corresponding Italian ones.

1. I'd like two packets of tissues.
2. How much is the chewing gum?
3. Have you got stamps?
4. I'd like five of them.
5. Do you sell cigarettes?
6. Let's buy some postcards.

a. Ne vorrei cinque.
b. Vendete sigarette?
c. Vorrei due pacchetti di fazzolettini.
d. Quanto costano i chewing-gum?
e. Compriamo delle cartoline.
f. Ha dei francobolli?

ACTIVITY 8

Roberto has bought one packet of tissues, two packets of chewing gum, three postcards, and three stamps. Look at **lo scontrino**, the till receipt, and see what's wrong.

CARTOLINE	4
FRANCOBOLLI	4
GIORNALI	2
FAZZOLETTINI	1
CHEWING-GUM	2

ACTIVITY 9

On the recording, listen to a cashier listing a number of purchases as he processes them at the till. Write down the quantity and price of each item.

____ CARTOLINE   ____

____ FAZZOLETTINI   ____

____ BOTTIGLIA D'ACQUA ____

____ CHEWING GUM   ____

____ GIORNALE   ____

ACTIVITIES 10 and 11 are on the recording.

ACTIVITY 12 is on the recording.

DIALOGUE 5.3
- Buongiorno. Vorrei vedere una borsa da viaggio.
- Grande o piccola?
- Piccola.
- Abbiamo questa in pelle, bellissima. Duecento euro. Le piace?
- Mi piace, ma non è per me, è un regalo. E vorrei spendere meno.
- È per un uomo o una donna?
- È per una ragazza.
- Questa in tessuto impermeabile è praticissima e conveniente.
- Quanto costa?
- C'è lo sconto del 30 per cento. Costa 55 euro.
- Va bene. La prendo.

VOCABULARY

la borsa da viaggio	travel bag
grande	big
piccolo/-a	small
la pelle	leather
bellissimo/-a	very beautiful, lovely
le piace?	do you (*formal*) like it? (*literally* does it please you?)
me	me
il regalo	gift
spendere	to spend
l'uomo (*m*)	man
la donna	woman
la ragazza	girl, young woman
il tessuto	fabric
impermeabile	waterproof
praticissimo/-a	very practical
conveniente	cheap
lo sconto	discount
per cento	per cent
lo/la	it

- The phrases **le piace?** (do you like *it*?) and **mi piace** (I like *it*) appear in the dialogue. To ask 'do you like *them*?', use **le piacciono?** and for 'I like *them*', say **mi piacciono**.
- You've also heard the expression **per me** (for me), where **me** is the pronoun* used with prepositions* (**con me** 'with me', **a me** 'to me', etc.). Have a look at the table to see how all the pronouns of this type behave.

per me	for me	**per noi**	for us
per te	for you – informal	**per voi**	for you – plural
per lei	for you – formal	**per loro**	for them
per lui/lei	for him/her		
per esso/-a	for it		

You'll have come across *la prendo*, meaning 'I'll take it' where **la** (it) is a pronoun replacing **la borsa**, a feminine* noun*. If the '*it*' replaced a masculine* noun, you'd say *lo prendo* and for plurals* '*them*' would be *li prendo/le prendo*.

ACTIVITY 13

Match the English phrases with their Italian equivalents.

1. It's a gift for you.
2. I'll take it.
3. I'd like to see some bags.
4. I don't want to spend that much.
5. I like the first one.
6. There's a discount.

a. Voglio spendere meno.
b. È un regalo per te.
c. C'è lo sconto.
d. Lo prendo.
e. Vorrei vedere delle borse.
f. Mi piace la prima.

ACTIVITY 14

Anna has seen a selection of four bags in a shop. Listen to her comments on the recording and, for each bag, mark whether or not she's interested.

1) YES ☐ NO ☐ 3) YES ☐ NO ☐

2) YES ☐ NO ☐ 4) YES ☐ NO ☐

ACTIVITIES 15 and 16 are on the recording.

Unit 5 · SHOPPING

ACTIVITY 17 is on the recording.

DIALOGUE 5.4

- Buongiorno. Posso dare un'occhiata?
- Certo. Se ha bisogno di me sono qui.

[…]

- Quanto costano questi pantaloni neri?
- Settanta euro.
- Ci sono altri colori?
- Ci sono anche questi rossi. Le piacciono?
- Preferisco quelli neri. Posso provarli?
- Certo.

[…]

- Come vanno? La taglia è giusta?
- No, sono grandissimi. Ha la taglia più piccola?
- Che taglia vuole?
- Questa è la 46, può portarmi la 44?
- Vado a vedere se l'abbiamo.

VOCABULARY

dare un'occhiata	to browse, to look around
certo	certainly
se	if
ha bisogno di (verb avere bisogno di)	you (*formal*) need (to need)
i pantaloni	trousers
nero/-a	black
il colore	colour
rosso/-a	red
preferisco (verb preferire)	I prefer (to prefer)
provarli (verb provare)	to try them on (to try on)
come vanno?	how are they?, how do they fit?
la taglia	size
giusto/-a	right
grandissimo/-a	very large big
che	what, which
portare	to bring

> - You'll have spotted that **grandissimi** rather than **molto grandi** was used to mean 'very big'. This is how adjectives* like **grande**, **bello**, etc. are intensified.
> - You'll also see that you say **posso provarli?** to ask 'can I try *them* on?' where the pronoun* **li** is attached to the verb* **provare**. You can also say **li posso provare?** Another such pronoun is **mi**, which means '(to) me': **può portarmi la 44?** 'could you bring me the 44?'. The other related pronouns work like this: **portarti** (bring you *informal*), **portargli** (bring him), **portarle** (bring her/you *formal*), **portarci** (bring us), **portarvi** (bring you *plural*), **portargli** (bring them).

ACTIVITY 18

Match the English with the Italian equivalents.

1. Can I have a browse?
2. How much are the black trousers?
3. Can I try them on?
4. Have you got the smaller size?
5. Are there other colours?
6. I'll take them.

a. Ha la taglia più piccola?
b. Posso dare un'occhiata?
c. Quanto costano i pantaloni neri?
d. Li prendo.
e. Posso provarli?
f. Ci sono altri colori?

ACTIVITY 19

Anna's in a clothes shop. Fill the gaps in her conversation with the shop assistant, **la commessa**

Anna: Posso dare _____ ?
Commessa: Sì, se ha _____ di me sono qui.
Anna: Quanto _____ questa gonna?
Commessa: 40 _____ .
Anna: Questa _____ troppo grande. Ha la taglia _____ piccola?
Commessa: Sì. _____ preferisce nera o rossa?
Anna: La _____ rossa.

ACTIVITIES 20 and 21 are on the recording.

Culture

Shopping in Italy is many people's dream. Copying with differences in the language, the units of measurement and the currency all at once might make the experience a bit daunting at first. But you'll find that it can be good fun too.

You can buy delicious food at **il supermercato** (supermarket), at **il mercato** (market), and of course in **un negozio** (shop). Here are just a few of the shops you'll come across: **la panetteria** (the bakery); **la macelleria** (the butcher's), **il verduraio** (the greengrocer's) where you'll find **la frutta** and **la verdura** (fruit and vegetables). **L'alimentari** (*m*) (the grocer's) sells nearly everything: **il pane** (bread), **il latte**, **il prosciutto**, **il sale** (salt), **l'olio**, **l'acqua**, **il vino**. The shop specializing in wine is **il vinaio** or, if you're after a more sophisticated selection, **l'enoteca** (*f*) where you can also sit and sample the wines before buying.

When shopping for **l'abbigliamento** (*m*) (clothes) and **le scarpe** (shoes), you'll be spoilt for choice. Whether you're looking for something **da donna** (for women), **da uomo** (for men), or **per bambini** (for children), you'll find shops to suit every taste and budget, from designer labels to cheap market finds. Sizes for shoes and clothes are different from the UK and US and you'll find useful conversion charts in the fold-out phrasefinder accompanying the course. Use **ho la taglia/ho il numero ...** (I'm size/I'm shoe size …) to say what size you are.

But beware – the Italian policy on refunds is quite different from that in Britain and the US. If you buy something, you can't take it back and get a refund. You may occasionally be able to exchange the item for another size or colour, but there's never a refund for items bought in the **saldi** (sales).

In Italy, there's no special licence required to sell alcohol so you can buy beer, wine and **liquori** (spirits) at the grocer's. On the other hand, you'll only find cigarettes on sale at **il tabaccaio** (tobacconist's), and in bars or newsagents displaying a big **T** sign outside. You can buy stamps at **il tabaccaio** as well as at **l'ufficio postale** (*m*) (the post office).

ACTIVITY 22

You want to buy a few things for lunch. Other than in a **supermercato** or **alimentari**, where else would you find them? Match the items and shops.

LE SIGARETTE	LA PANETTERIA
LA CARNE	IL VINAIO
I FUNGHI	IL VERDURAIO
IL VINO	IL TABACCAIO
IL PANE	IL MACELLAIO

ACTIVITY 23

On the recording, listen to a shopper buying some shoes and then answer the questions below in English.

1) What colour are the shoes she's seen in the shop window, **in vetrina**?

2) How much are the shoes?

3) What shoe size is she?

4) Are the shoes available in her size?

5) What size does she end up trying?

6) Does she buy the shoes?

Review 5

1. You're shopping at the 'alimentari'. Fill in the gaps.

a. Vorrei _____ _____ di latte. (2 l)
b. Vorrei _____ _____ di prosciutto. (200 g)
c. Vorrei _____ _____ di pane. (1 kg)
d. Vorrei _____ _____ d'olio. (1 l)
e. Vorrei _____ _____ di olive. (100 g)
f. Vorrei _____ _____ d'acqua. (6 bottles)

2. Match the English and Italian phrases.

1. Have you got some tissues?
2. How much are these postcards?
3. Do you sell stamps?
4. Three stamps for the US.
5. Where are the foreign magazines?

a. **Quanto costano queste cartoline?**
b. **Vendete francobolli?**
c. **Ha dei fazzolettini?**
d. **Tre francobolli per gli Stati Uniti.**
e. **Dove sono i giornali stranieri?**

3. Someone's buying a present. Put the sentences in the right order.

– Certo. Quanto vuole spendere?
– Posso vedere quella rossa?
– Vorrei vedere delle borse. Devo fare un regalo.
– 90, 100 euro.
– Il colore non mi piace tanto. Ne avete altre?
– Questa blu le piace?
– Un attimo, vado a prenderla.
– Abbiamo la stessa borsa in nero. Oppure in rosso ma è più grande.

Time to listen

4. On the recording, listen to someone going through their shopping list. Can you circle the items they're going to buy?

acqua	olive
birra	panini
caffè	parmigiano
carne	riso
insalata	sale
latte	succo d'arancia
mozzarella	vino
olio	zucchini

5. On the recording, listen to someone in a shop trying on a pair of trousers and circle the correct answers.

1. How do the trousers fit?
    a. The trousers are a little big.
    b. They're a little small.
    c. They're perfect.
2. How does the next size he tries on fit?
    a. The next size he tries on is fine.
    b. There isn't a bigger size available.
    c. The next size he tries on is too small.
3. Does he like the trousers?
    a. He likes the trousers.
    b. He doesn't like the trousers.
    c. He's not sure.

Unit 5 · SHOPPING

Time to talk

6. You're now going to take part in a conversation. Prepare what you are going to say using the prompts. Then, when you're ready, do the activity on the recording.

(Say 'I'd like a bottle of water and some tissues.')
– Una bottiglia piccola o grande?
(Say 'Small.')
– Altro?
(Say 'Yes, I'd like a packet of chewing gum.')
– Questi vanno bene?
(Say 'Yes, they're fine.')
– Altro?
(Ask 'How much are these postcards?')
– Settanta centesimi.
(Say 'I'll take five of them')
(Ask 'Have you got stamps?')
– No, mi dispiace. Deve andare dal tabaccaio.
(Ask 'How much is it?')

7. Now test your progress in Unit 5. How would you say:

a. I'd like 100 grams of cured ham.
b. Have you got some red wine?
c. I'd like four stamps for Great Britain.
d. Do you sell tissues?
e. Can I have a browse?
f. Can I see the trousers in the window?
g. Is there a discount?
h. Is there a bigger size?
i. I'll take it.

You can check your answers on the recording.

Unit 6

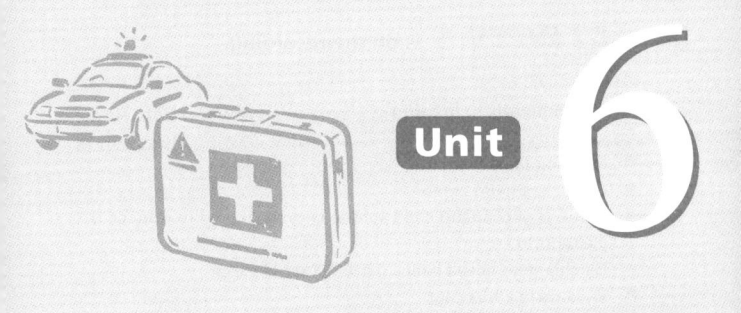

Emergencies

In this unit you will learn how to:

- ask for help
- report a theft to the police
- ask for a doctor or an ambulance
- explain that your car has broken down
- explain that you've missed your plane

Once you've got the opportunity to put your Italian into practice, just go ahead and do it and don't worry about getting things wrong. People will still be able to understand you. They'll also appreciate the fact that you're making the effort to speak their language and they'll be more receptive. Above all, enjoy learning to communicate in Italian!

Unit 6 · EMERGENCIES

ACTIVITY 1 is on the recording.

DIALOGUE 6.1
- Mi hanno rubato lo zaino.
- Quando è successo?
- Mezzora fa, al mercato.
- Cosa c'era nello zaino?
- Tutto. Il portafoglio con i soldi e la carta di credito e anche il passaporto.
- Ha chiamato la sua banca per bloccare la carta?
- Sì, la carta è bloccata.
- Ora deve fare la denuncia del furto in questura. Ha avvertito il consolato?
- Ancora no.
- Il consolato può esserle d'aiuto per i documenti e se ha bisogno di soldi.

VOCABULARY

mi hanno rubato … (verb rubare)	my … has/have been stolen (*literally* they've stolen … from me) (to steal)
lo zaino	rucksack
è successo (verb succedere)	it happened (to happen)
mezzora fa	half an hour ago
c'era	there was
tutto	everything
il portafoglio	purse, wallet
i soldi (*plural*)	money
la banca	bank
bloccare	cancel
fare la denuncia	to make a statement
il furto	theft
la questura	police station
ha avvertito (verb avvertire)	you have notified (to notify)
il consolato	consulate
ancora no	not yet
esserle d'aiuto	to be of help to you (*formal*)

Unit 6 · EMERGENCIES

(!)

Most of the events in the dialogue have just taken place.
mi *hanno rubato* lo zaino = my rucksack has been stolen
ha *chiamato* la sua banca? = *have* you *called* your bank?
ha *avvertito* il consolato? = *have* you *notified* the consulate?
These are examples of the perfect tense* in Italian. This tense is used to refer to recent events as above. Note that you could also say in English 'my rucksack was stolen', 'did you call your bank?' and 'did you notify the consulate?' because a wider variety of past tenses may be used to translate the Italian perfect. It's mostly formed using the auxiliary verb* **avere** and the past participle* of the main verb. With **succedere**, **essere** and verbs of motion such as **andare**, **partire**, etc., the Italian auxiliary verb **essere** + past participle is used:
quando *è successo*? = when did it happen?
***siamo stati* a Roma** = we were in Rome
***sono andato* a Firenze** = I went to Florence
***è partito* un'ora fa/ieri** = he left an hour ago/yesterday.

ACTIVITY 2

Match the English and Italian phrases.

1. My bag has been stolen.
2. I haven't cancelled my credit card.
3. Her purse has been stolen.
4. Has your passport been stolen too?
5. When did it happen?

a. Non ho bloccato la carta di credito.
b. Quando è successo?
c. Mi hanno rubato la borsa.
d. Le hanno rubato il portafoglio.
e. Le hanno rubato anche il passaporto?

ACTIVITY 3

Someone's reporting a theft. Fill in the gaps in the conversation.

– Cosa è _____ _____, signorina?
– Ci hanno _____ gli zaini.
– Cosa _____ negli zaini?
– I _____, 300 euro in tutto. E _____ i documenti.

ACTIVITIES 4 and 5 are on the recording.

Unit 6 · EMERGENCIES

ACTIVITY 6 is on the recording.

DIALOGUE 6.2

- Può aiutarmi per favore? Ho bisogno di un medico.
- Cosa ha fatto?
- Mio figlio è caduto e si è fatto male.
- Vuole chiamare l'ambulanza? Vuole andare all'ospedale?
- No, non c'è bisogno. Non è grave, si è solo fatto male alla spalla. Però vorrei vedere un dottore.
- La guardia medica è qui vicino. Vi porto io in macchina.

VOCABULARY

può aiutarmi? (verb aiutare)	can you help me? (to help)
il medico	doctor
il figlio/la figlia	son/daughter
è caduto (verb cadere)	he fell (to fall)
si è fatto male	he hurt himself
l'ambulanza (*f*)	ambulance
l'ospedale (*m*)	hospital
non c'è bisogno	there's no need
grave	serious
la spalla	shoulder
però	but
il dottore/la dottoressa	doctor
la guardia medica	doctor on duty (eg in holiday resort)
vi porto (verb portare)	I'll take you (*plural*) (to take/transport)
in macchina	by car

- In this and the previous dialogue, you'll have seen the verb* **fare** which means 'to do' or 'to make'.

(io)	**faccio** I do	(noi)	**facciamo** we do
(tu)	**fai** you do (*informal*)	(voi)	**fate** you do
(lui/lei; lei)	**fa** he/she/it does; you do (*formal*)	(loro)	**fanno** they do

Unit 6 · EMERGENCIES

> - You'll also have seen that you use **vi porto** to say 'I'll take *you*' (plural). To say 'I see *you*' (plural), you'd use **vi vedo**. Similarly, 'I see her' would be **la vedo** and 'I see *you*' (singular) **ti vedo**. The table below gives the full list of these pronouns*. Check out the notes on pp 79–81 where some of these pronouns (**lo/la** and **li/le**) were introduced.
>
> | | | | |
> |---|---|---|---|
> | you see *me* | **mi vedi** | you see *her/it* | **la vedi** |
> | I see *you* (informal) | **ti vedo** | you see *us* | **ci vedi** |
> | I see *you* (formal) | **la vedo** | I see *you* (plural) | **vi vedo** |
> | you see *him/it* | **lo vedi** | I see *them* | **li/le vedo** (m/f) |
>
> - These words can be attached to the verb if this is an infinitive*: **può aiutarmi?** means 'can you help *me*?'. Note that in this case the final **-e** of the infinitive is dropped. Look at the grammar section for a full summary of pronouns.

ACTIVITY 7

Fill in the gaps to complete the statements and questions.

Può _____?	(Can you help us?)
Ho _____ di _____ .	(I need a doctor.)
Voglio _____ l'_____ .	(I want to call an ambulance.)
_____ l'_____ ?	(Where's the hospital?)
Può _____ all'ospedale?	(Can you take him to the hospital?)
Vorrei _____ subito un _____ .	(I'd like to see a doctor right away.)

ACTIVITY 8

There's been an accident. Put the sentences below in the right order.

a) È grave?
b) Sì, è grave, deve andare subito all'ospedale.
c) Può chiamare l'ambulanza?
d) Mia figlia si è fatta male.
e) Telefono subito. Cosa è successo?

ACTIVITIES 9 and 10 are on the recording.

Unit 6 · EMERGENCIES

🎧 **ACTIVITY 11** is on the recording.

DIALOGUE 6.3
- Scusi, può aiutarci? Abbiamo un guasto alla macchina.
- Che problema c'è?
- Non lo so. Forse un guasto al motore. La macchina non parte.
- Non è finita la benzina?
- No, abbiamo fatto il pieno ieri.
- L'officina del meccanico è chiusa, apre dopo pranzo. Se potete aspettare, alle due mando il carro attrezzi. Dov'è la macchina?
- L'abbiamo lasciata al parcheggio di piazza da Vinci.
- Chi è il proprietario?
- Io. Le do il mio nome, il numero di cellulare e il numero di targa dell'auto.

VOCABULARY

abbiamo un guasto alla macchina	our car has broken down
non lo so (verb sapere)	I don't know (to know)
forse	maybe
il motore	engine
parte (verb partire)	starts (to start, *literally* to go)
è finita (verb finire)	it's run out (*literally* to finish)
la benzina	petrol, gas
fare il pieno	to fill up
ieri	yesterday
l'officina (f)	garage
il meccanico	car mechanic
chiuso/-a	closed
apre (verb aprire)	it opens (to open)
dopo pranzo	after lunch
aspettare	to wait
carro attrezzi	breakdown truck, tow truck
do (verb dare)	I'll give (to give)
l'abbiamo lasciata (verb lasciare)	we left it (to leave)
il parcheggio	car park, parking lot
chi	who

VOCABULARY

il/la proprietario/-a — owner
il numero di targa — number plate

> You'll have seen the question word* **chi?** ('who?') in the dialogue: **chi è il proprietario?** 'who is the owner?'. To ask questions like 'who are you going with?' or 'who is it for?' in Italian, you put the preposition* at the beginning: **con chi vai?** and **per chi è?** You'll remember this from the note on **quale?** ('which?') in Unit 4. To ask the question 'whose?', you say **di chi?: di chi è questa macchina?** 'whose car is this?'; to answer it, say **è di Roberto** 'it's Roberto's' or **è mia** 'it's mine'.

ACTIVITY 12

Match the questions with the appropriate answers.

1. Avete un guasto alla macchina?
2. C'è la benzina?
3. Di chi è quell'auto?
4. Dov'è la macchina?
5. Può mandare il carro attrezzi?
6. C'è un'officina qui vicino?
7. Qual è il numero di targa?

a. Sì, ma è chiusa.
b. Lo mando subito.
c. Sì, non parte.
d. Sì, ho fatto il pieno.
e. È di Tom.
f. A147GUDX
g. In un parcheggio.

ACTIVITY 13

Listen to dialogue 6.3 again and mark the following true or false.

1. Their car has broken down.   TRUE/FALSE
2. They have a flat tyre.   TRUE/FALSE
3. The car is making a strange noise.   TRUE/FALSE
4. They've run out of petrol.   TRUE/FALSE
5. The garage is closed for lunch.   TRUE/FALSE
6. The breakdown truck is on its way.   TRUE/FALSE
7. They've left the car in a car park.   TRUE/FALSE

ACTIVITIES 14 and 15 are on the recording.

ACTIVITY 16 is on the recording.

DIALOGUE 6.4
- Può aiutarmi per favore, ho perso l'aereo.
- Dove deve andare?
- A Milano. E da Milano domattina presto ho la coincidenza per San Francisco.
- A che ora parte il volo per San Francisco domattina?
- Alle sette.
- Purtroppo stasera non ci sono più voli per Milano. Il suo era l'ultimo. E domattina il primo è alle sette e mezzo.
- Non è colpa mia. Ho fatto tardi perché c'era un incidente sull'autostrada. Ora come faccio?
- Le consiglio di prendere un treno notturno per Milano. Buona fortuna!

VOCABULARY

ho perso (verb perdere)	I've missed (to miss) (*flight*)
Milano	Milan
domattina	tomorrow morning
presto	early
la coincidenza	connection
il volo	flight
purtroppo	unfortunately
stasera	tonight
non ci sono più …	there are no more …
era	(it) was
non è colpa mia	it's not my fault
ho fatto tardi	I was late
perché	because; *also* why
l'incidente (*m*)	accident
ora come faccio?	what can I do now?
consiglio (verb consigliare)	I'd advise (to advise)
il treno notturno	night train
buona fortuna!	good luck!

ACTIVITY 17

Match the phrases in English with their Italian equivalents.

1. I've missed the plane.
2. Are there other flights tonight?
3. It's not my fault.
4. You've missed the connection.
5. We were late.

a. Ha perso la coincidenza.
b. Abbiamo fatto tardi.
c. Ci sono altri voli stasera?
d. Non è colpa mia.
e. Ho perso l'aereo.

ACTIVITY 18

You're calling a friend to let her know that you've missed your flight. Fill in the gaps to complete the telephone conversation.

– _____ ?

– Ciao Anna, sono Roberto.

– Ciao Roberto. _____ sei?

– _____ all' _____ . Ho _____ l'aereo.

– Cosa? Sei ancora a Palermo?

– Purtroppo sì.

– Cosa è _____ ?

– _____ è _____ mia. Il treno per l'aeroporto era in _____ . Arrivo _____ .

– Ciao, a domattina.

ACTIVITIES 19 and 20 are on the recording.

Culture

Whether you want **la polizia** or **i Carabinieri** (the police), **i vigili del fuoco** (the fire brigade), an ambulance or just someone to come to your aid, the word to shout in an emergency is **aiuto!** (help!). In the case of a theft, you can call out **al ladro!** (stop thief!) or if there's a fire, **l'incendio** (*m*), shout **al fuoco!** (fire!)

Before you go to Italy, it's a good idea to familiarize yourself with the different emergency numbers, just to be on the safe side:

112 – **Carabinieri pronto intervento** (emergency police service)
113 – **soccorso pubblico di emergenza** (general emergencies)
115 – **vigili del fuoco** (fire brigade)
118 – **ambulanza** (ambulance)

For medical emergencies, you might need to go to the **pronto soccorso** (A&E, ER) at the nearest hospital. In holiday resorts there's often a **guardia medica** (doctor on duty) on site. If you feel ill, say **sto male**. If you've hurt yourself in some way, use **mi sono fatto/-a male**. Here are some of the most common ailments that you might need to describe in Italian:

ho mal di testa	I have a headache
ho mal di pancia/stomaco	I have a stomach-ache
ho mal di denti	I have (a) toothache
ho mal di gola	I have a sore throat
ho il mal di mare	I feel seasick
mi fa male una gamba/un occhio	my leg/eye hurts
ho la diarrea	I have diarrhoea
ho la nausea	I feel sick
ho la febbre/il raffreddore/la tosse	I have a temperature/ a cold/a cough

Unit 6 · EMERGENCIES

If you're planning to drive in Italy, make sure you find out what to do in case of a breakdown or an accident before you set off. Recovery procedures and costs vary from country to country.

Whether the car is your own or a rented one, **a noleggio**, check that documents such as your driving licence, **la patente**, and your insurance policy, **l'assicurazione** (*f*), are in order.

ACTIVITY 21

On the recording, some people need help. Circle the right emergency service (or possibly services) to contact.

1. Who does she need?
   a) la polizia
   b) l'ambulanza
   c) i vigili del fuoco
2. Who does he need?
   a) la polizia
   b) l'ambulanza
   c) i vigili del fuoco
3. Who does she need?
   a) la polizia
   b) l'ambulanza
   c) i vigili del fuoco
4. Who does he need?
   a) la polizia
   b) l'ambulanza
   c) i vigili del fuoco

ACTIVITY 22

Your friend is ill and can't speak Italian. Translate for him.

– I feel ill.

– _____

– I have a headache and a stomach-ache.

– _____

– I feel sick.

– _____

Review 6

1. Your bag with your passport, cards and money was stolen while you were on the bus. You're telling a policeman about it. Can you answer his questions?

– Cosa è successo?
– _____

– Dov'è successo?
– _____

– Cosa c'era nella borsa?
– _____

– Deve bloccare le carte di credito. Ha chiamato la banca?
– _____

– Bene, ora deve fare la denuncia.
– _____

– In questura.

2. Match the phrases in English and Italian.

1. Can you help us?
2. My son feels very ill.
3. I need an ambulance.
4. I must take him to the A&E.
5. I don't have a car.

a. **Devo portarlo al pronto soccorso.**
b. **Non ho la macchina.**
c. **Ho bisogno di un'ambulanza.**
d. **Mio figlio sta molto male.**
e. **Può aiutarci?**

3. Some people need help. For each emergency, choose the appropriate piece of advice.

1. Mi hanno rubato il portafoglio.
2. Ho avuto un grave incidente.
3. Siamo in ritardo per l'aereo.
4. Un ragazzo sta male.
5. C'è un incendio al campeggio.

a. Chiamate l'ambulanza.
b. Chiamate i vigili del fuoco.
c. Chiamate la polizia.
d. Chiamate l'aeroporto.
e. Chiamate il medico.

Time to listen

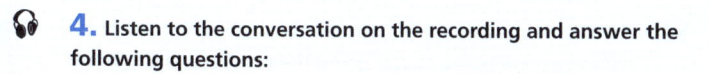

4. Listen to the conversation on the recording and answer the following questions:

1. What's happened?
2. Where does he want to go?
3. Are there direct flights to his final destination?
4. Where does the connection leave from?
5. What time can he leave at?

5. A woman is talking to a car mechanic on the phone. Listen to the conversation and circle the correct statements.

1. Why is she calling the mechanic?
   a. Her car has broken down.
   b. She has run out of petrol.
   c. She's had an accident.
2. What does she do?
   a. She takes the car to the garage.
   b. She stays where she is.
   c. She takes the bus home.
3. What happens next? Can the mechanic help?
   a. No, he can't help as he hasn't got a breakdown truck.
   b. Yes, he sends a breakdown truck
   c. No, so she calls another garage.
4. Where is she now?
   a. She's in Milan.
   b. She doesn't know where she is.
   c. She's in Milano Square.

Time to talk

6. You're now going to take part in a conversation. Prepare what you are going to say using the prompts. Then, when you're ready, do the activity on the recording.

(Ask 'Can you help me?')
– Cosa è successo?
(Say 'My purse has been stolen.')
– Chi è stato?
(Say 'I don't know. What can I do now?')
– Deve bloccare le carte di credito.
(Say 'Yes, I must call the bank.')
– E poi deve fare la denuncia.
(Ask 'Where do I have to go?')
– In questura.
(Say 'Thank you very much.')
– Prego.

7. Now test your progress in Unit 6. How would you say:

a. Help!
b. I need help.
c. We need an ambulance.
d. I feel ill.
e. My rucksack has been stolen.
f. Do you want to call the police?
g. I want to cancel the credit cards.
h. We've had an accident.
i. My car has broken down.
j. We've missed the plane.

You can check your answers on the recording.

Answer key

Unit 1
Activity 2
1. Arrivederci signora.
2. Buonasera.
3. Ciao.
4. Buonanotte.
5. Arrivederci signor Paoli.
6. Salve.
7. Buongiorno signorina.
8. Ciao Anna.

Activity 4
1b; 2d; 3a; 4c

Activity 8
1c; 2a; 3d; 4b

Activity 9
sono; sei; siamo; è; è; è; siete; sono

Activity 14
1. FALSE; 2. TRUE; 3. TRUE; 4. FALSE; 5. TRUE; 6. FALSE; 7. FALSE

Activity 15
1. britannici;   2. canadese;
3. americani;   4. italiane;
5. australiano;   6. francesi

Activity 19
1d; 2e; 3a; 4b; 5c; 6f

Activity 20
1. Non vive a Venezia.
2. Loro non abitano in Scozia.
3. Non siamo americani.
4. Non ho capito.
5. Liz non è qui in vacanza.
6. Non si chiamano Hemshall.

Activity 23
1. INFORMAL;   2. FORMAL;
3. INFORMAL;   4. INFORMAL

Activity 24
è; italiano; del; ti; tu

Review 1
1 1g; 2d; 3e; 4b; 5a; 6h; 7c; 8f
2 1d; 2c; 3e; 4b; 5a; 6f
3 Mi chiamo George, sono americano e abito a New York.
   Mi chiamo Caroline, sono inglese e abito a Londra.
   Mi chiamo Claudia, sono italiana e abito a Venezia.
   Mi chiamo Tom, sono scozzese e abito a Edimburgo.
   Mi chiamo Dan, sono australiano e abito a Sydney.
4 mi chiamo; lei; buongiorno; mi chiamo; dov'è; inglese; dove; vivo; a; abito.
5 1c; 2a; 3c

Unit 2
Activity 3
1d; 2e; 3b; 4f; 5c; 6a

Activity 4
1a; 2b; 3c; 4a

Activity 8
1c; 2a; 3b; 4e; 5d

Activity 9
un'; due; due; venti; caffè; quattro; tè; un

Activity 13
1d; 2a; 3b; 4c

Activity 14
a) il riso; il pesce; gli spinaci
b) i ravioli; l'aragosta; none

Activity 18
1d; 2e; 3a; 4f; 5b; 6c

Activity 19
Può portare il conto?
Sì, subito.
Posso pagare con la carta di credito?
No, mi dispiace.

Activity 22
No, there are 4 mistakes in the bill. It should be:

2 COPERTI	1,60
1 VINO – BIRRA	7,50
1 ACQUA MINERALE	2,00
2 ANTIPASTI	6,00
2 PRIMI	16,00
2 SECONDI	18,00
1 CONTORNI	4,00
2 CAFFÈ – LIQUORI	5,00
TOTALE	60,10

Activity 23
un; freddo; tè; al; per

Review 2
1 1g; 2h; 3e; 4a; 5c; 6d; 7b; 8f
2 1c; 2e; 3a; 4b; 5f; 6d
3 Vuole ordinare?
Sì. Cosa consiglia come primo?
I ravioli sono freschi.
Prendo i ravioli.
E come secondo? Abbiamo carne o pesce.
Vorrei una bistecca.
Come contorno ci sono spinaci o insalata mista.
Gli spinaci.
Cosa vuole bere?
Vino bianco e acqua gassata.
4 cosa; succo; bicchiere; un; hai; sete
5 1c; 2a; 3b

Unit 3
Activity 2
Ha una camera singola?
Quanto costa a notte?
Scusi, come si scrive? OR Come si scrive, scusi?
La colazione è compresa.
Vorrei prenotare una camera.

Activity 3
1 FALSE; 2 TRUE; 3 FALSE; 4 FALSE

Activity 7
1c; 2a; 3d; 4b

Activity 8
1 TRUE; 2 FALSE; 3 FALSE; 4 FALSE

Activity 12
1e; 2a; 3d; 4c; 5b

Activity 17
1b; 2d; 3a; 4c

Activity 18
funziona; riesco; mandare; altra

Activity 21
desidera; chiamo; un problema; riesco a; ho; non; numero; errore

Review 3
1 1c; 2b; 3e; 4g; 5a; 6d; 7f
2 1c; 2e; 3b; 4a; 5d
3 una; vicino; la; è; costa; indirizzo; prego
4 1 FALSE; 2 TRUE; 3 FALSE; 4 TRUE; 5 FALSE; 6 TRUE
5 1b; 2c; 3a

Unit 4
Activity 2
1b; 2a; 3d; 4c

Activity 3
1 TRUE; 2 FALSE; 3 TRUE; 4 FALSE

Activity 7
1d; 2a; 3e; 4b; 5g; 6c; 7f

Activity 8
yes; yes; bus no. 2; opposite the church

Activity 12
andare; a; deve; semaforo; a; devo; girare; cartello

Activity 13
1b; 2b; 3a

ANSWER KEY

Activity 17
1) Sono le quattordici e venti OR le due e venti.
2) Il film comincia alle ventuno e trenta OR alle nove e mezzo.
3) Arrivo alle sedici OR alle quattro (di pomeriggio).
4) L'autobus parte alle dieci e quaranta OR alle undici meno venti.

Activity 18
1 FALSE; 2 TRUE; 3 FALSE; 4 FALSE

Activity 21
on the first floor, on the left

Activity 22
parla; no; un; a

Activity 23
b. She's at the station.

Review 4
1. 1c; 2f; 3d; 4e; 5a; 6b
2. 1c; 2b; 3f; 4e; 5d; 6a
3. metropolitana; quale; prendere; linea; a quale
4. 1c; 2b; 3c; 4a
5. 1 FALSE; 2 TRUE; 3 FALSE; 4 FALSE; 5 TRUE; 6 TRUE

Unit 5

Activity 2
due etti; prosciutto crudo; un etto; parmigiano
mezzo chilo di panini
un litro di latte

Activity 3
pears: 1 kg; grapes: ½ kg; oil: a bottle; mushrooms: 300 g; courgettes/zucchinis: 5; cheese: 100g; bread: ½ kg

Activity 7
1c; 2d; 3f; 4a; 5b; 6e

Activity 8
4 postcards rather than 3; 4 stamps rather than 3; 2 magazines when he hasn't bought any

Activity 9
5 CARTOLINE 2 euro e 50
1 pacchetto di FAZZOLETTINI 50 centesimi
1 BOTTIGLIA D'ACQUA 1 euro
1 pacchetto di CHEWING-GUM 30 centesimi
1 GIORNALE 3 euro e 50

Activity 13
1b; 2d; 3e; 4a; 5f; 6c

Activity 14
1 NO; 2 NO; 3 NO; 4 YES

Activity 18
1b; 2c; 3e; 4a; 5f; 6d

Activity 19
un'occhiata; bisogno; costa; euro; è; più; la; preferisco; rossa

Activity 22
LE SIGARETTE — IL TABACCAIO
LA CARNE — IL MACELLAIO
I FUNGHI — IL VERDURAIO
IL VINO — IL VINAIO
IL PANE — LA PANETTERIA

Activity 23
1) red 2) 67 euros 3) 37½ 4) no 5) 38 6) yes

Review 5
1. a) due litri; b) due etti; c) un chilo; d) un litro; e) un etto; f) sei bottiglie

2 1c; 2a; 3b; 4d; 5e

3 1) Vorrei vedere delle borse. Devo fare un regalo.
2) Certo. Quanto vuole spendere?
3) 90, 100 euro.
4) Questa blu le piace?
5) Il colore non mi piace tanto. Ne avete altre?
6) Abbiamo la stessa borsa in nero. Oppure in rosso ma è più grande.
7) Posso vedere quella rossa?
8) Un attimo, vado a prenderla.

4 they are going to buy:
acqua
caffè
carne
insalata
latte
mozzarella
panini
riso
succo d'arancia
vino

5 1b; 2a; 3b

Unit 6

Activity 2
1c; 2a; 3d; 4e; 5b

Activity 3
successo; rubato; c'era; soldi; anche

Activity 7
aiutarci; bisogno; un dottore (OR un medico); chiamare; ambulanza; dov'è; ospedale; portarlo; vedere; dottore (OR medico)

Activity 8
1 c; 2 e; 3 d; 4 a; 5 b

Activity 12
1c; 2d; 3e; 4g; 5b; 6a; 7f

Activity 13
1 TRUE; 2 FALSE; 3 FALSE; 4 FALSE; 5 TRUE; 6 FALSE; 7 TRUE

Activity 17
1e; 2c; 3d; 4a; 5b

Activity 18
pronto; dove; sono; aeroporto; perso; successo; non; colpa; ritardo; domattina

Activity 21
1c; 2b; 3b and also a; 4a

Activity 22
Sto male.
Ho mal di testa e mal di pancia (OR di stomaco).
Ho la nausea.

Review 6

1 – *Cosa è successo?*
– Mi hanno rubato la borsa
– *Dov'è successo?*
– Sull'autobus.
– *Cosa c'era nella borsa?*
– Il passaporto, le carte di credito e i soldi.
– *Deve bloccare le carte di credito. Ha chiamato la banca?*
– Sì.
– *Bene, ora deve fare la denuncia.*
– Dove faccio la denuncia?
– *In questura.*

2 1e; 2d; 3c; 4a; 5b

3 1c; 2a AND c; 3d; 4e OR a; 5b

4 1) He missed his plane
2) Glasgow
3) There are no direct flights to Glasgow
4) London
5) 15:10

5 1a; 2b; 3b; 4c

Vocabulary

	a	at, in; to
	a che ora ...?	(at) what time ...?
	a destra	(on the) right
	a noleggio	rented
	a notte	per night
	a piedi	on foot
	a sinistra	(on the) left
	abbastanza	enough
l'	abbigliamento (*m*)	clothing
	abitare	to live
	accettare	to accept
l'	acqua (*f*)	water
l'	aereo (*m*)	plane
l'	aeroporto (*m*)	airport
	aiutare	to help
l'	aiuto (*m*)	help
	aiuto!	help!
	al, allo, all', alla *etc*.	see a
	al fuoco!	fire!
	al ladro!	stop thief!
l'	albergo (*m*)	hotel
l'	alimentari (*m*)	grocer's
l'	alta stagione (*f*)	high season
	altro/-a	other; different; extra
un/un'	altro/altra	another; a different; an extra
	altro?	anything else?
l'	ambulanza (*f*)	ambulance
	americano/-a	American
	anche	also, too
	ancora no	not yet
	andare	to go
l'	antipasto (*m*)	starter
	appena	just
	aprire	to open
l'	aragosta (*f*)	lobster
l'	arancia (*f*)	orange
l'	aranciata (*f*)	orangeade
	archeologico/-a	archaeological
l'	aria condizionata (*f*)	air conditioning
	arrivare	to arrive, to come, to get to
	arrivederci	goodbye

VOCABULARY

l'	**arrivo** (m)	arrival
	aspettare	to wait
l'	**assicurazione** (f)	insurance
l'	**attimo** (m)	moment
	attivato/-a	switched on (*of an alarm*)
	australiano/-a	Australian
l'	**autista** (m/f)	driver
l'	**auto** (f)	car
l'	**autobus** (m)	bus
l'	**autostrada** (f)	motorway, freeway
	avere	to have
	avere bisogno (di)	to need
	avvertire	to notify
il	**bagno**	bathroom
il/la	**bambino/-a**	child
la	**banca**	bank
il	**bar** (m)	bar
la	**bassa stagione**	low season
	basta così	that's all (*in shop*)
	bellissimo/-a	very beautiful, lovely
	bello/-a	beautiful
	ben attrezzato/-a	well equipped
	bene	fine, well
la	**benzina**	petrol, gasoline
	bere	to drink
il	**bicchiere**	glass
il	**biglietto**	ticket
il	**binario**	platform, track
la	**birra**	beer
la	**bistecca**	steak
	bloccare	to cancel
	blu	blue
la	**borsa**	bag
la	**borsa da viaggio**	travel bag
la	**bottiglia**	bottle
la	**brioche**	croissant
	britannico/-a	British
	buona fortuna!	good luck!
	buonanotte	goodnight
	buonasera	good evening; goodbye (*in the evening*)
	buongiorno	hello, good morning
	buono/-a	nice; good
	cadere	to fall

VOCABULARY

il	caffè	(espresso) coffee
il	caffè decaffeinato	decaffeinated coffee
il	caffè lungo	black coffee slightly diluted
il	caffè macchiato	espresso with a dash of milk
	caldo/-a	hot
la	camera	(bed)room
il	campeggio	campsite, campground
il	camping	campsite, campground
	canadese	Canadian
	capire	to understand
il	cappuccino	cappuccino
i	Carabinieri (*plural*)	police
la	carne	meat
	caro/-a	expensive
la	carota	carrot
il	carro attrezzi	breakdown truck; tow truck
la	carta di credito	credit card
la	carta d'identità	identity card
il	cartello	sign
la	cartolina	postcard
	c'è	there is
il	cellulare	mobile phone
la	cena	dinner
il	centesimo	cent
il	centro informazioni turistiche	tourist information office
	c'era	there was
	cercare	to look for
	certamente	certainly
	certo	certainly
	che	what, which
	che ore sono?	what time is it?
i	chewing-gum (*plural*)	chewing gum
	chi	who
	di chi	whose
	chiamare	to call
	chiamarsi	to be called
la	chiave	key
la	chiesa	church
il	chilo	kilo
	chiuso/-a	closed
	ci	there; (to) us
	ci sono	there are
	ciao	hi, hello; bye

VOCABULARY

la	cioccolata calda	hot chocolate
la	città	town, city
la	coca	Coke®, Coca-Cola®
il	cognome	surname
la	coincidenza	(train/plane) connection
la	colazione	breakfast
il	colore	colour
	come	as; how
	come?	pardon?
	come ci arrivo?	how do I get there?
	come si scrive?	how do you spell it?
	come stai/sta?	how are you? (*informal/formal*)
	come ti chiami/si chiama?	what's your name? (*informal/formal*)
	cominciare	to start, to begin
il/la	commesso/-a	shop assistant
	comprare	to buy
	compreso/-a	included
	con	with
	consigliare	to recommend; to advise
il	consolato	consulate
la	consumazione al tavolo	(charge for) eating/drinking at the table
il	conto	bill, check
il	contorno	side dish
	controllare	to check
	conveniente	cheap
il	coperto	cover charge
il	corso	avenue
la	cosa	thing
	cosa?	what?
	crema	cream; custard
	crudo/-a	cured (*of ham*)
il	cuscino	pillow
	da	from; at (*somebody's place*)
	da donna	for women (*of clothes, shoes*)
	da uomo	for men (*of clothes, shoes*)
	dal, dallo, dall', dalla *etc.*	see da
	dall'altra parte	on the other side
	dare	to give
	dare un'occhiata	to browse, to look around
	davanti a	in front (of), opposite
il	decaffeinato	decaffeinated coffee
	del, dello, dell', della *etc.*	some; see also di
la	denuncia	statement (*at police station*)

il	depliant	leaflet
il	deposito bagagli	left luggage (facility)
	desidera?	can I help you? (*in shop*)
	destra	right
	di	of, from
	di dove sei?	where are you from? (*informal*)
	di fronte a	in front (of), opposite
la	diarrea	diarrhoea
	dica	can I help you? (*in shop*)
il/la	disabile	disabled person
	disattivato/-a	switched off (*of an alarm*)
la	doccia/-ce	shower
il	documento	document, proof of ID
	domattina	tomorrow morning
	domenica	Sunday
	domenica notte	Sunday night
la	donna	woman
	dopo	after
	doppio/-a	double
il/la	dottore/dottoressa	doctor
	dove	where
	dov'è?	where is he/she/it?
	dovere	to have to, must
	dritto	straight on
	e	and
	ecco a lei	here you are (*formal*)
l'	edicola (*f*)	newsstand
	Edimburgo	Edinburgh
l'	enoteca (*f*)	vintage wine store/wine bar
l'	errore (*m*)	mistake, error
	esatto/-a	correct
	essere	to be
	esso/-a	it
l'	etto(grammo) (*m*)	100 grams
l'	euro (*m*)	euro
	fa	ago
	fame: ho fame	hunger: I'm hungry
	fare	to do, to make
	fare il pieno	to fill up (*at petrol/gas station*)
	fare tardi	to be late
la	farmacia	chemist's, pharmacy
	farsi male	to hurt oneself, to injure oneself
il	fazzolettino	tissue

VOCABULARY

la	febbre	(high) temperature (*when ill*)
la	fermata	stop (*on bus, underground route*)
il/la	figlio/-a	son/daughter
	finire	to finish
	fino a	up to
	Firenze	Florence
la	focaccia	flat salted bread
il	formaggio	cheese
	forse	maybe
	fra	between, among; in (*in time phrases*)
	francese	French; Frenchman/woman
il	francobollo	stamp
	freddo/-a	cold
	fresco/-a	fresh
la	frutta	fruit
il	fungo	mushroom
	funzionare	to work (*of TV, machine, etc.*)
	fuori	outside
il	furto	theft
il	gabbiano	seagull
il	gabinetto	toilet
	gallese	Welsh; Welshman/woman
la	gamba	leg
	gassato/-a	sparkling
il	gelato	ice-cream
il	giornalaio	newsagent's
il	giornale	newspaper; magazine
il	giorno	day
	giovedì	Thursday
	girare	to turn
	giusto/-a	right
	gli	the; (to) him; to them
la	gola	throat
la	gonna	skirt
la	Gran Bretagna	Great Britain
	grande	big, large
	grandissimo/-a	very large
	grave	serious
	grazie	thanks
	grazie mille	thanks very much
la	guardia medica	doctor on duty; first-aid station
il	guasto	breakdown; fault (*in car*)
	ha, hai, hanno, *etc.*	see **avere**

VOCABULARY

l'	hotel (m)	hotel
	i	the (*plural, masculine*)
	ieri	yesterday
	impermeabile	waterproof
	impiegare	to take (*speaking of time taken*)
	in	in; by (*car*)
	in fondo	at the back, at the end
	in orario	on time
	in ritardo	late
	in tutto	in total
l'	incendio (m)	fire
l'	incidente (m)	accident
l'	incrocio (m)	crossroads, junction
l'	indirizzo (m)	address
l'	infermeria (f)	first-aid room
l'	Inghilterra (f)	England
	inglese	English, British; Englishman/woman
l'	insalata mista (f)	mixed salad
	invece di	instead of
	io	I
	irlandese	Irish; Irishman/woman
	italiano/-a	Italian
	l'	the; you (*formal*); her; him; it
	la	the; you (*formal*); her; it
	là/lì	there
	lasciare	to leave (behind)
il	latte	milk
	le	the; to you (*formal*); to her; them
	lei	you (*formal*); she; her
	lentamente	slowly
	li	them
il	limone	lemon
la	linea	line
la	linea esterna	outside line
il	liquore	liqueur
i	liquori	spirits
il	litro	litre
	lo	him; it
	Londra	London
	lontano/-a	far
	loro	they; them; their; theirs
la	luce	light
	lui	he; him

VOCABULARY

	lunedì	Monday
il	macchiato	espresso with a dash of milk
la	macchina	car
la	macelleria	butcher's
la	maionese	mayonnaise
il	mal di denti	toothache
il	mal di gola	sore throat
il	mal di mare	seasickness
il	mal di pancia/stomaco	stomach-ache
il	mal di testa	headache
	mandare	to send
	mangiare	to eat
il	mare	sea
	martedì	Tuesday
la	mattina	morning
	me	me
il	meccanico	car mechanic
il	medico	doctor
	meno	minus; less
il	mercato	market
	mercoledì	Wednesday
il	metro	metre
la	metropolitana	underground, subway
la	mezza pensione	half board
la	mezza stagione	midseason
	mezzanotte	midnight
	mezzo/-a	half
	mezzogiorno	midday
la	mezzora	half an hour
	mi	(to) me
	mi dispiace	I'm sorry
	mi piace/piacciono	I like it/them
	Milano	Milan
il	mini-market	mini-market
il	minuto	minute
	mio/-a, miei/mie	my; mine
	molto	very (much)
	molto/-a	a lot of
	molti/-e	lots of, many
il	monte	mountain
il	motore	engine
il	museo	museum
	naturale	still (*of mineral water*)

VOCABULARY

la	nausea	sickness, nausea
	ne	of it/them
	né	neither
il	negozio	shop
	nel, nello, nell', nella *etc.*	see in
	nero/-a	black
	no	no
	noi	we; us
	non	not
	non … più	not … any more
	non c'è male	not too bad (*describing how one is*)
	non è colpa mia	it's not my fault
	non ho capito	I don't understand
	non lo so	I don't know
	non si preoccupi	don't worry
	nostro/-a	our; ours
la	notte	night
il	numero	number
il	numero di targa	number plate
il	numero di telefono	telephone number
l'	occhio (*m*)	eye
l'	officina (*f*)	garage (*for car repairs*)
	oggi	today
l'	olio (*m*)	oil
l'	oliva	olive
l'	ora (*f*)	hour
	ora	now
	ordinare	to order
l'	ospedale (*m*)	hospital
l'	ostello della gioventù (*m*)	youth hostel
il	pacchetto	packet
il	paese	village; country
	pagare	to pay
il	pane	bread
la	panetteria	bakery
il	panino	roll
i	pantaloni	trousers, pants
il	parcheggio	car park, parking lot
	parlare	to talk, to speak
il	parmigiano	parmesan cheese
la	partenza	departure
	partire	to leave, to go; to start (*of car*)
il	passaporto	passport

VOCABULARY

la	patente	driving licence
la	pelle	leather; skin
la	pensione	B&B, guest house
la	pensione completa	full board
	per	for, to
	per cento	percent
	per favore	please
la	pera	pear
	perché	because; why
	perdere	to lose; to miss (*bus, plane etc.*)
	però	but
il	pesce	fish
il	pezzetto	small piece
il	pezzo	piece
	piacere!	pleased to meet you!
il	piano	floor
la	piazza	square
la	piazzola	pitch, site (*for tent*)
	più	more
la	pizza	pizza
	poi	then
la	polizia	police
il	pomeriggio	afternoon
il	portafoglio	purse, wallet
	portare	to bring, to take
	potere	to be able to, can
il	pranzo	lunch
	praticissimo/-a	very practical, very handy
	preferire	to prefer
il	prefisso	area telephone code
	prego	you're welcome
	prego?	can I help you? (*in bar, shop*)
	prendere	to have (*drink*); to take, to catch (*bus, train etc.*); to take (*right/left*)
	prenotare	to book
	prenotato/-a	booked
	presto	early
la	prima colazione	breakfast
il	primo (piatto)	first course
il	problema	problem
	pronto?	hello? (*on the phone*)
il	pronto soccorso	A&E, ER
il/la	proprietario/-a	owner

VOCABULARY

	proprio	right
il	prosciutto	ham
	proseguire	to keep going
	provare	to try (on)
	purtroppo	unfortunately
	quale, qual	which, what
	qual è l'indirizzo?	what's the address?
	qualcosa	something
	qualcuno	somebody
	quando	when
	quanto … ?	how much … ?; how long … ?
	quant'è?	how much is it (in total)?
	quanto ci vuole?	how long does it take?
	quanto costa/costano?	how much is it/are they?
il	quarto	quarter
	quello/-a	that, that one
	questo/-a	this, this one
la	questura	police station
	qui	here
	qui vicino	nearby
il	raffreddore	cold
il/la	ragazzo/-a	boy/girl, young man/woman
il	regalo	gift
	regolare	to regulate
	ripetere	to say again
il	riso	rice
	riuscire	to be able to; to succeed
	Roma	Rome
	rosso/-a	red
la	rotonda	roundabout, traffic circle
	rubare	to steal
	sabato	Saturday
i	saldi	sales
il	sale	salt
	salve	hello
	San, Santo/-a	saint
	sapere	to know; to be able to
	sbagliare	to get wrong
	sbagliare strada	to be on the wrong road
le	scarpe	shoes
	scendere	to get off
lo	sconto	discount
lo	scontrino	till receipt

VOCABULARY

la	Scozia	Scotland
	scozzese	Scottish; Scotsman/woman
	scremato/-a	skimmed (*of milk*)
	scrivere	to write; to spell
	scusi	excuse me; sorry
	se	if
il	secondo	main course
	sei	see essere
la	sera	evening
	sete: ho sete	thirst: I'm thirsty
	sì	yes
	si è fatto/-a male	he's hurt himself; she's hurt herself
	si fa prima	it's quicker
	siamo completi	we're full
	siamo, siete	see essere
la	signora	madam; Mrs; lady
il	signore	sir; Mr; gentleman
la	signorina	Miss; young lady
	singolo/-a	single
	sinistra	left
i	soldi (*plural*)	money
	solo	only
	soltanto	only
	sono	see essere
la	spalla	shoulder
	spendere	to spend (*money*)
	spero di sì	I hope so
gli	spiccioli (*plural*)	small change
gli	spinaci (*plural*)	spinach
lo	spuntino	snack
	stamattina	this morning
	stanotte	tonight
	stasera	this evening
la	stanza	room
	stare male	to feel ill
gli	Stati Uniti	United States
la	stazione	(railway) station
la	strada	street, road, way
	straniero/-a	foreign
	su	on; by
	subito	straight away, immediately
	succedere	to happen
il	succo	juice

VOCABULARY

il	succo d'arancia	orange juice
	sul, sullo, sull', sulla *etc.*	see su
	sul mare	by the sea
	suo/-a, suoi/sue	your; yours (*formal*); her, hers; his
il	supermercato	supermarket
la	sveglia	alarm (clock)
il	tabaccaio	tobacconist's
la	taglia	size
	tanto	very (much), really
	tanto/-a	a lot of
	tanti/-e	lots of
	tardi	late
	te	(to) you (*informal*)
	tè	tea
	telefonare	to telephone
il	telefono	telephone
la	tenda	tent
il	tessuto	fabric
	ti	(to) you (*informal*)
la	tisana	herbal tea
il	toast	toasted sandwich
la	toilette	toilet
il	tonno	tuna
	tornare indietro	to go back, to turn back
la	tosse	cough
il	totale	total
	tra	between, among; in (*in time phrases*)
il	tramezzino	sandwich
il	treno	train
il	treno notturno	night train
	troppo/-a	too (much)
	trovare	to find
	tu	you (*singular, informal*)
	tuo/-a, tuoi/tue	your (*informal*); yours (*informal*)
	tutto	everything, all
la	TV	TV
l'	ufficio postale (*m*)	post office
	ultimo/-a	last; last (one)
	un, uno, una, un'	a
l'	uno/una	each
	un po' (di)	some
	un po' di meno	a bit less
	un po' di più	a bit more

l'	uomo	man
l'	uva (*singular*)	grapes
	va bene	that's fine, OK
la	vacanza	holiday, vacation
	in vacanza	on holiday, on vacation
	vedere	to see
	vegetariano/-a	vegetarian
	vendere	to sell
	venerdì	Friday
	Venezia	Venice
	venire	to come, to go
la	verdura (*singular*)	vegetables
il	verduraio	greengrocer's
	verso	around; towards
la	vetrina	shop window
	vi	(to) you (*plural*)
la	via	street, road
	vicino	near, nearby
i	vigili del fuoco (*plural*)	fire brigade
il	vinaio	wine store
il	vino	wine
	vivere	to live
	voi	you (*plural*)
	volere	to want
il	volo	flight
	vorrei	I'd like
	vostro/-a	your (*plural*); yours (*plural*)
lo	zafferano	saffron
lo	zaino	rucksack
lo	zucchero	sugar
lo	zucchino	courgette, zucchini (*sing.*)

Grammar Section

This section explains those grammatical terms marked with an asterisk in the body of the course. It also provides summary tables and information about a number of points of grammar.

Adjective

A word that describes a noun or pronoun, giving information about a quality: colour, size, nationality, etc. Examples are **buono** (good, nice), **rosso** (red), **grande** (big), **americano** (American).
Adjectives often have different endings, taking the same gender (masculine/feminine) and number (singular/plural) as the noun and pronoun they describe. Compare:
lui è **americano** (he's American) and *lei* è **americana** (she's American);
la camera è **grande** (the room is big) and *le camere* **sono grandi** (the rooms are big).
Note that, in the singular, adjectives like **grande** have the same ending for masculine and feminine (*la camera/l'albergo è grande*).

Agree

To match another word in number (singular or plural), gender (masculine or feminine) or pronoun (I, you, he, we, etc).

Article ➡ Definite article, Indefinite article

Auxiliary verb

In English, a verb which, together with a main verb, is used to form a particular tense of the main verb, e.g. in 'I *have booked* a table', the auxiliary verb is 'have' and forms the perfect tense of the main verb 'to book'. English auxiliary verbs are also used to form questions, or negative statements. In Italian there are two auxiliary verbs, **avere** and **essere**, which are used to form compound tenses such as the perfect tense e.g. ***Ho prenotato* un tavolo.**

Cardinal numbers

These are numbers such as **uno**, **due**, **tre**, **quattro** etc. (one, two, three, four, etc.), rather than **primo**, **secondo**, **terzo**, **quarto** etc. (first, second, third, fourth, etc.) which are ordinal numbers.

Conjugation ➡ Verb conjugation tables p. 128

A verb takes different forms according to its subject: *io* (I), *tu* (you – *singular, informal*), *lui* (he), etc. This process of verb change is known as conjugation: *io* abito, *tu* abit*i*, *lui* abita etc. In Italian, verbs are categorized in three main conjugations, according to their endings in the infinitive: **-are** (abitare, andare etc.), **-ere** (vendere, vivere etc.) or **–ire** (capire, riuscire etc.) Many verbs follow the patterns of conjugation very closely (see 'Regular verbs'). Other verbs (andare, volere, riuscire etc.), while belonging to one or other of the conjugations, have forms and tenses which don't follow the standard patterns. See also 'Irregular verbs'.

Consonants

In the Italian alphabet, these are: **b, c, d, f, g, h, l, m, n, p, q, r, s, t, v, z**.
J, k, w, and **x** are only used in words of foreign origin.
Consonant sounds are described in the Pronunciation section p. 6.

Definite article

The definite article ('the' in English) is used before a noun when referring to something which has been mentioned already: **il** treno (*the* train). Italian has many forms of the definite article as it changes according to the gender and number of the noun it precedes and is also affected by the letter the noun begins with.

	singular	plural	examples
masculine	**il** *before most consonants*	**i**	il treno, i treni
	lo *before* **gn, ps, z,**		
	or **s**+ *consonant*	**gli**	lo spuntino, gli spuntini
	l' *before vowels*	**gli**	l'aereo, gli aerei
feminine	**la** *before consonants*	**le**	la pensione, le pensioni
	l' *before vowels*	**le**	l'aragosta, le aragoste

Direct object

A word or phrase which is immediately affected by the action indicated by the verb: vorrei **un caffè** (I'd like *a coffee)*; **lo** prendo (I'll take *it*).

Ending

A letter (or letters) added to nouns and adjectives which indicates their number and gender. The endings added to a verb show the subject, number, and tense of that verb.

i vin*i* italian*i*   (Italian wines)
io abit*o*, noi abit*iamo*   (I live, we live)

Feminine ➡ Gender

One of the two genders in Italian.

Gender

There are two genders in Italian, which means that nouns are either masculine or feminine. Words such as articles and adjectives must agree in gender with the nouns they refer to. Compare *un* **uomo** *italiano*/*una* **donna** *italiana* (An Italian man/an Italian woman).
Similarly, pronouns must reflect the gender of the nouns they replace. Dov'è Anna? La vedi? (Where's *Anna*? Can you see *her*?)

Indefinite article

The indefinite article (*a* or *an* in English) varies in Italian depending on whether the noun it is used with is masculine or feminine.

	singular	examples
masculine	un	un treno, un albergo
	uno before gn, ps, z, or s+ *consonant*	uno zucchino, uno spuntino
feminine	una	una birra, una pera
	un' before vowels	un'arancia, un'ora

Indirect object

The noun, pronoun or phrase indirectly affected by the action of the verb (compare with 'direct object'):
le do il mio numero (I'll give *you* my number)
può portarmi la taglia 44? (could you bring *me* size 44?)

Infinitive

The infinitive is the basic form of the verb. It doesn't indicate a particular tense or person and in Italian the infinitive endings -are, -ere, or -ire are used to categorize verbs in conjugations.
mangiare (to eat), bere (to drink), capire (to understand), essere (to be), andare (to go).
The infinitive is the verb form usually given in dictionaries.

Intonation

The pattern of sounds made in a statement or a question as the speaker's voice rises and falls.

Irregular verb

A verb which, although it falls into one of the three conjugations in Italian, does not follow the standard patterns of verb formation for verbs ending in -are, -ere, -ire. Some pronouns (I, you, he, etc.) and tenses will produce different forms. In Italian, essere (to be), avere (to have), andare (to go), fare (to do/make) are all classed as irregular verbs.

Masculine ➡ Gender

One of the two genders in Italian.

Negative

A negative sentence asserts that something is not the case. To make a sentence negative in Italian, you just put **non** (meaning 'not') before the *verb*. Compare:
sono irlandese/**non** sono irlandese (I'm Irish/I'm not Irish)
loro *abitano*/loro **non** *abitano* a Roma (They live/They don't live in Rome)

Noun

A noun is used to name a person, an animal, an object, a concept, etc. A noun in Italian has a gender. It can be masculine – un panino (a bread roll) or feminine – una stanza (a room). A noun has a number. It can be singular – un panino, una stanza or plural – due panini, due stanze.

Number

Nouns and pronouns can be singular or plural. Words such as articles and adjectives must agree in number with the nouns and pronouns they refer to. Compare *una gonna rossa* (a red skirt) and *due* gonn*e* ross*e* (two red skirts); *io* sono americano (I'm American) and *noi* siamo americani (we're American).

Ordinal numbers

These are the numbers such as **primo/-a**, **secondo/-a**, **terzo/-a**, **quarto/-a**, etc. (first, second, third, fourth, etc.), rather than uno, due, tre, quattro etc. (one, two, three, four, etc.) which are the cardinal numbers. Note that they behave like adjectives.

Partitive article

A small word in Italian which is placed before nouns to express an indefinite number or quantity of something, e.g. **dell**'acqua (**some** water), **dei** giornali (**some** magazines). Like the definite and indefinite articles, the partitive article will vary according to the gender, number and initial letter of the noun it refers to.

Past participle

The form of the verb used in combination with the verbs avere or essere in tenses such as the perfect. The link with the infinitive of the verb may be more or less visible in the past participle:

capito (understood)	from	capire	(to understand)
successo (happened)	from	succedere	(to happen)
stato (been)	from	essere	(to be)

Perfect tense ➡ Tenses

Person

A category used to distinguish between I/we (1st person), you (2nd person) and he/she/it/they (3rd person) forms of the verb. The person is reflected in the verb form and/or in the pronoun accompanying it.
mangio (I eat) –1st person singular
il treno è in orario (the train is on time) – 3rd person singular
noi abitiamo a Roma (we live in Rome) – 1st person plural

Plural ➡ Number

One of the two categories of grammatical number.
Here's how the change from the singular to the plural for most Italian nouns and adjectives is reflected in their endings:

	singular	plural	examples
masculine	in -o	change to -i	il treno, i treni
			italiano, italiani
	in -e	change to -i	il bicchiere, i bicchieri
			inglese, inglesi
feminine	in -a	change to -e	la camera, le camere
			italiana, italiane
	in -e	change to -i	la pensione, le pensioni
			inglese, inglesi

Some nouns don't change in the plural, i.e. those ending in an accented vowel il caffè/i caffè, la città/le città, in a consonant il bar/i bar, and exceptions such as euro: 1 euro/2 euro. There are also irregular plurals such as la mano/le mani (the hand/the hands).

Possessive adjectives

Possessive adjectives are used with a noun and show ownership. In Italian, they are usually preceded by the definite article and they agree in person with the owner, and in gender and number with the 'possession' as underlined in the examples:

il mio passaporto (**my** passport), *le tue chiavi* (**your** keys) whether the owner is male or female.

	masc.	fem.		masc.	fem.
my sing.	il mio	la mia	plural	i miei	le mie
your (*informal*)	il tuo	la tua		i tuoi	le tue
his/her/its	il suo	la sua		i suoi	le sue
your (*formal*)	il suo	la sua		i suoi	le sue
our	il nostro	la nostra		i nostri	le nostre
your	il vostro	la vostra		i vostri	le vostre
their	il loro	la loro		i loro	le loro

Preposition

A preposition is used before a noun or a pronoun to indicate its relationship to another word in the sentence. This relationship can give information about direction, position, sequence, etc. In some cases a preposition has a purely grammatical role.

una camera **con** bagno (a room **with** bathroom)
in orario (**on** time)
il treno **per** Firenze (the train **to** Florence)

Pronoun

A pronoun is used to replace a noun. The pronoun can be masculine or feminine, singular or plural and may refer to people, things or concepts.
io sono Roberto e **tu**? (**I**'m Roberto, who are **you**?)
queste cartoline sono belle, **le** prendo (these postcards are nice, I'll take **them**).

Pronouns can be subjects:

	SINGULAR	PLURAL	
io	I	noi	we
tu	you (*informal*)	voi	you
lui	he	loro	they
lei	she/you (*formal*)		
esso/-a	it		

Subject pronouns are generally omitted in Italian (unless they are needed for emphasis) as the subject is indicated by the verb ending.

Note that there are three words for **you** in Italian.
tu/lei/voi:

- tu   singular, informal 'you' when talking to a friend, a child or a member of the family
- lei   singular formal 'you', when talking to somebody you don't know very well (but remember that lei also means 'she').
- voi   plural 'you', when talking to more than one person, formally and informally.

Pronouns can be direct objects:

SINGULAR		PLURAL	
mi	me	ci	us
ti	you (*informal*)	vi	you
lo	him/it (*m*)	li	them (*m*)
la	her/you (*formal*)/it (*f*)	le	them (*f*)

Pronouns can be indirect objects:

SINGULAR		PLURAL	
mi	to me	ci	to us
ti	to you (*informal*)	vi	to you
gli	to him/it (*m*)	gli	to them
le	to her/you(*formal*)/it (*f*)		

Pronouns can be used with prepositions (such as con, per, a, etc.):

SINGULAR		PLURAL	
me	me	noi	us
te	you (*informal*)	voi	you
lui	him	loro	them
lei	her/you (*formal*)		
esso/-a	it		

Question words ➡ Questions

Questions

Usually a question in Italian is formed in the same way as a statement. The only thing which distinguishes the two is the rising intonation of the voice at the end of a question. Compare:
tu sei Anna (you're Anna) and tu sei Anna? (are you Anna?);
abitano a Roma (they live in Rome) and abitano a Roma? (do they live in Rome?). English relies heavily on the verb **do** to form questions but note that there is no equivalent in Italian.

When you ask a question to find out who, where, when, how, how much, etc., you use the relevant Italian question word – chi, dove, quando, come, quanto, etc. Question words are immediately followed by the verb in Italian:
come ti chiami? (what's your name?)
di dove siete? (where are you from?)
quanto costa? (how much is it?)
qual è la fermata? (which stop is it?)

Regular verb

A verb which follows closely one of the standard patterns of verb conjugation. In Italian, abit**are** (to live), am**are** (to love), parl**are** (to speak/talk) are regular verbs in the first conjugation of **-are** verbs.

Singular ➡ Number

One of the two categories of grammatical number. The singular is the basic form of nouns or adjectives given in dictionaries.

Subject

The subject of a verb performs the action indicated by the verb. It can be a noun or a pronoun.
il **film** comincia alle 9 (the **film** starts at 9 o'clock)
In Italian it doesn't need to be explicit (in the form of a pronoun) as it does in English.
io abito a Londra or abit*o* a Londra (**I** live in London)
piove (**it**'s raining)

Stress

The syllable of a word receiving relatively greater force or emphasis than the other(s) is said to be the *stressed* syllable, e.g. **city** (cit**tà** in Italian).

Syllable

Any of the units into which a word is divided, containing a vowel sound and usually one or more consonants (lon-ta-no, te-le-fo-no).

Tenses

The action, process or state of affairs expressed by a verb can be happening now: in this case the verb is in the *present tense*. If something has already happened, the verb will be in the *past tense* and if it has not yet taken place or is only planned, the verb will be in the *future*.

The *present tense* is very useful and will be sufficient in a lot of situations:
abitano a New York (they live in New York);
prendo un caffè (I'll have a coffee)
cerchiamo un albergo (we're looking for a hotel)

The Italian *perfect tense* (one of the Italian past tenses) describes events that have recently taken place and it can be translated with a wider variety of English *past tenses*. It's mostly formed using the *auxiliary verb* **avere** together with the *past participle* of the main verb, although with essere, succedere and verbs of motion such as andare, partire, etc. the *auxiliary verb* **essere** + *past participle* is used:
ho capito (I understand)
mi **hanno rubato** lo zaino (my rucksack has been stolen)
abbiamo perso l'aereo (we missed the plane)
and
quando **è successo**? (when did it happen?)
sono andato a Firenze (I went to Florence)
è partito un'ora fa/ieri (he left an hour ago/yesterday)

Verb

A word or phrase used to express an action, a process or a state of affairs:
cerchiamo un campeggio (we're looking for a campsite)
piove (it's raining)
il treno è in ritardo (the train's late)

Vowels

In the Italian alphabet, these are **a**, **e**, **i**, **o**, **u**. (**Y** is only used in words of foreign origin). When a word begins with a vowel, the word preceding it might be affected.
Compare la birra (the beer) and l'acqua (the water), dove sono? (where are they?) and dov'è? (where is it?).
Vowel sounds are described in the Pronunciation section p. 5.

Italian verb conjugations

1 essere
io sono
tu sei
lui/lei è
noi siamo
voi siete
loro sono

2 avere
io ho
tu hai
lui/lei ha
noi abbiamo
voi avete
loro hanno

Regular verbs

3 abitare
io abito
tu abiti
lui/lei abita
noi abitiamo
voi abitate
loro abitano

4 vendere
io vendo
tu vendi
lui/lei vende
noi vendiamo
voi vendete
loro vendono

5 partire
io parto
tu parti
lui/lei parte
noi partiamo
voi partite
loro partono

6 capire*
io cap*isco*
tu cap*isci*
lui/lei cap*isce*
noi capiamo
voi capite
loro cap*iscono*

*A number of verbs, such as capire, have a slightly different conjugation but are still considered to be regular.

Irregular verbs

7 volere
io voglio
tu vuoi
lui/lei vuole
noi vogliamo
voi volete
loro vogliono

8 dovere
io devo
tu devi
lui/lei deve
noi dobbiamo
voi dovete
loro devono

9 potere
io posso
tu puoi
lui/lei può
noi possiamo
voi potete
loro possono

10 andare
io vado
tu vai
lui/lei va
noi andiamo
voi andate
loro vanno

11 bere
io bevo
tu bevi
lui/lei beve
noi beviamo
voi bevete
loro bevono

12 dare
io do
tu dai
lui/lei dà
noi diamo
voi date
loro danno

13 fare
io faccio
tu fai
lui/lei fa
noi facciamo
voi fate
loro fanno

14 prendere
io prendo
tu prendi
lui/lei prende
noi prendiamo
voi prendete
loro prendono

15 piacere
mi/ti/gli/etc.   piace
mi/ti/gli/etc.   piacciono